D1082782

A Taste of Freedom

A Taste
of Freedom

A Cookbook With Recipes
and Remembrances
From the Hampton Institute

Carolyn Quick Tillery

CITADEL PRESS
Kensington Publishing Corp.
www.kensingtonbooks.com.

CITADEL PRESS BOOKS are published by

Kensington Publishing Corp.
850 Third Avenue
New York, NY 10022

All Kensington titles, imprints, and distributed lines are available at special quantity discounts for bulk purchases for sales promotions, premiums, fund-raising, educational, or institutional use. Special book excerpts or customized printings can also be created to fit specific needs. For details, write or phone the office of the Kensington special sales manager: Kensington Publishing Corp., 850 Third Avenue, New York, NY 10022, attn: Special Sales Department, phone 1-800-221-2647.

First printing: April 2002

10 9 8 7 6 5 4 3 2

Printed in the United States of America

Library of Congress Control Number: 2001098718

ISBN 0-8065-2321-2

Dedicated to the memory of my parents,
Senior Master Sergeant (Ret.) John Gordon Quick
and
Delores Adam Quick

CONTENTS

PREFACE

A Taste of Freedom is a historic cookbook and companion piece to *The African-American Heritage Cookbook,* a recipe and remembrance book from Alabama's renowned Tuskegee Institute. Before there was a Tuskegee Institute, however, there was Hampton—a post–Civil War institute established for the education of newly freed slaves. It was here that a former slave by the name of Booker T. Washington was educated before he went on to found Tuskegee Institute, one of the premier historic black universities in the United States.

In 1866 General Samuel C. Armstrong, the son of missionaries, arrived at Fort Monroe in Virginia to accept an appointment as superintendent of the Bureau of Refugees, Freedmen and Abandoned Lands (Freedmen's Bureau at Fort Monroe). General Armstrong had previously served in the Union army in command of the Colored Cavalry Regiments and Battery B, Second U.S. Colored Light Artillery.

In three prophetic visions that Armstrong had experienced during the war, he saw the entire future design of the school he wanted to found for African-Americans. And on April 1, 1868, Hampton Normal and Agricultural School would open in a leftover barracks with two teachers and fifteen students.

For the thousands of newly freed slaves, Hampton became an oasis of opportunity. With the assistance of the American Mission Association, the school began training them to teach and lead their people. The earliest support for the institute came from the Freedmen's Bureau, Northern philanthropists, religious groups, and from the students themselves, who literally "sung up" Virginia Hall.

While *A Taste of Freedom* contains recipes for traditional southern mainstays such as fried chicken, potato salad, and greens, its primary focus is the elegant southern foods for which the Virginia coastal region is famous. Seafood, Virginia ham, condiments, pickles and preserves, as well as other mouthwatering recipes indigenous to the Hampton-Tidewater area distinguish this recipe and remembrance book from its predecessor.

Like *The African-American Heritage Cookbook,* this prequel contains stories and vintage photographs. The traditional recipes transcend time, while the narrative accompaniment makes time stand still in order that we might better experience historic moments. The narratives tell the story of the founding of Hampton, but this narrative cookbook also contains a larger history—the story of a bound people seeking freedom and the right to education and self-determination. Remarkably, the story of their bondage and their first steps toward freedom and education all begin right in the Hampton area, not far from where the "school by the sea" was founded.

The recipes, photographs, and stories here reflect the triumphant spirit of former slaves who helped free themselves and not only participated in the founding of a school, but assisted in the preservation of the Union.

Acknowledgments

Thanks to my family, J.R. and Ashley, for your love, support, and encouragement. Special thanks to my friend Cynthia Nelson Harrison, Hampton class of 1981. The author gratefully acknowledges the cooperation of Hampton University, the University archives, and the kind cooperation of assistant archivist, Donzella Maupin. The author further acknowledges the cooperation of the Casemate Museum. Thanks, too, to my Citadel editor, Margaret Wolf, and the staff at Kensington/Citadel.

Washington, D.C., Sept. 10, 1873

. . . I can not give an unbiased opinion of Hampton Institute, because from the commencement I have been its ardent and sanguine friend. I am now on its Board of Trustees, and eager to see this institution placed on solid foundations.

Hampton presents unity in its Board of Trustees, unity in its faculty of instruction, and able administration. It combines practical teaching with its theoretical, and opens avenues to the children of the poor. Its requirements are intelligence and industry, not limited by race or caste. I invoke upon it the favor and sympathy of men and women who love to do good, and repair some of the ills of our past national and social crimes.

God is sure to help its earnest workers. Let the catholic spirit of our divine Lord and Master never suffer it to be cramped by bigotry or narrowness, or cursed by skepticism. Then will this young and happy institute meet the warm wishes of its indefatigable superintendent, Gen. S. C. Armstrong, and not fail to fulfill the unflagging faith of its founders.

With many thanks for the honor you extend to me,

I remain sincerely your and General Armstrong's friend,

O. O. HOWARD,
President Howard University

THE BEGINNINGS OF HAMPTON

"Freedom Fort"

*"The year of 1861 opened with threats of trouble near at hand, and before
the spring had fairly set in, our civil war began . . ."*

—Mary Frances Armstrong, 1874, in *Hampton and Its Students*,
by Mary F. Armstrong and Helen W. Ludlow.

"The creek upon which Hampton stands was for a while the boundary-line between the two armies—the Union lines remaining intrenched *[sic]* upon its eastern shore during the early part of the war, while the combating forces swayed back and forth as fortune favored one or the other." This description is by Mary Frances Armstrong, the sister-in-law of Hampton Institute's founder, and the area she describes was the only place below the Mason and Dixon Line that never fell to the Confederacy during the Civil War.

Union troops occupied Fortress Monroe, located approximately two miles from the town of Hampton, where, as the story goes, three slaves belonging to Colonel Charles K. Mallory, a Hampton lawyer and Confederate union officer, came to Colonel Benjamin Franklin Butler, the commander of Fortress Monroe, seeking refuge. The slaves told Butler that Mallory had used them to construct the Confederate battery at Sewall's Point and planned to take them farther south to serve the Confederate cause.

Mallory sent an emissary, Major John B. Cary, to demand the return of the slaves under the Fugitive Slave Law. Butler, also trained in the law, shrewdly declared himself to be under no obligation to uphold the constitutional rights, namely property rights, of citizens of a foreign country. He added that if Mallory considered the slaves property, he, Butler, would hold them as "contraband of war since they are engaged in the construction of your battery and claimed as your property."

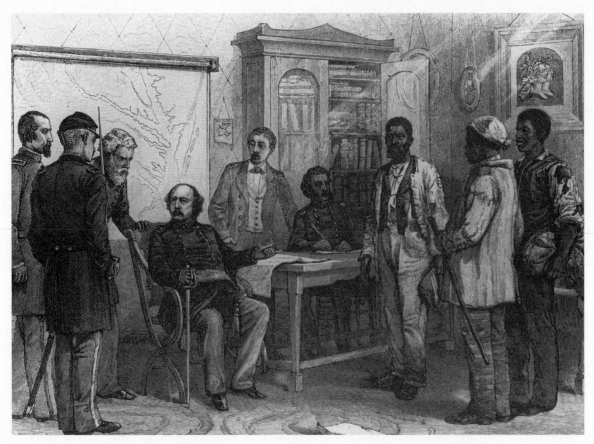

Three "Contraband" being questioned by General Butler at Fortress Monroe
(Courtesy of Casemate Museum, Hampton, Virginia)

Butler's bold pronouncement, which preceded the Emancipation Proclamation by eighteen months, was later confirmed by the War Department and referred to by Abraham Lincoln as "Butler's Fugitive Slave Law." News of it spread like wildfire and refugees, or "contraband," fled to Fortress Monroe in droves, "with their lives in their hands, as the Israelites of old," in the words of Mary Frances Armstrong. "Fortress Monroe and its guns offered tangible protection, and the spirit of the officers in command promised a surer protection still; so that in little squads, in families, singly, or by whole plantations, [they] flocked within [n]orthern lines, until the whole area of ground protected by the Union encampments was crowded by their hurriedly-built cabins of rudely-split logs."

"Contraband" coming into Fortress Monroe
(Courtesy of Casemate Museum, Hampton, Virginia)

Many African-Americans boasting strong roots in Hampton and the Tidewater area of Virginia descend from those slaves who dared to seek the refuge of Fortress Monroe during the Civil War. Within the fort's protection, they were no longer considered slaves, but beyond the area of Union control these "refugees" were still considered property, and were subject to recapture should they venture into Confederate territory. From the barricade of the protected stronghold they now called "Freedom Fort," these "refugees" immediately set about the business of helping one another. (Harriet Tubman was appointed chief nurse of the contraband hospital.) Serving as cooks, servants, carpenters, teamsters, laborers, and stevedores, these "contraband of war" assisted in the war effort, always casting a hopeful eye toward the future.

Slaves fleeing to Fortress Monroe
(Reproduced from the collections of the Library of Congress)

Freedom's Struggle

Though still considered property by the Confederates, these former slaves actively participated in a growing struggle that could result in their freedom, and with it the attendant right to education and self-determination. On Sunday, March 9, 1862, following an unresolved four-hour battle between the ironclad ships *Merrimac* (renamed CSS *Virginia*) and *Monitor*, the Confederate's *Merrimac* was still considered a menace to Federal gunboats, and the Union forces made plans to ram it with a steel prow.

When the *Arrago*, a merchant vessel, was fitted with a sharp steel prow, the assigned crew, surmising its purpose, deserted in a body. The quartermaster in charge of contraband at Fortress Monroe lined up 350 Negro stevedores, explained the situation, and called for volunteers to man the *Arrago*. The entire line stepped forward! Willing to lay down their lives, which by law, did not belong to them, they did not hesitate to heed duty's call. Before they could act, however, the *Merrimac* was scuttled by the Confederates on May 11, 1862, when they were forced to evacuate Norfolk. Later, when the Confederate forces were bombarded by the Federal army and navy, fourteen contraband faithfully and without panic worked the after-gun of the upper deck of the battleship *Minnesota* and hailed, with victors' pride, the Stars and Stripes as they waved again on the soil of the Carolinas.

Many contraband gave their lives in this struggle for freedom and self-determination. In so doing, they exemplified the spirit and foundation upon which General Armstrong would soon build Hampton Institute. In a short time these "refugees" would be called "freedmen."

Escaped slaves entering Fortress Monroe
(Courtesy of Casemate Museum, Hampton, Virginia)

The Freedmen's Village, Hampton, Virginia
(Reproduced from the collections of the Library of Congress)

In August 1861, the American Missionary Association sent the Rev. C. L. Lockwood as a missionary to the freedmen. Mary Frances Armstrong reports: "He found them, 'quartered in deserted houses, in cabins and tents, destitute and desolate . . . [with] a hunger for books among those who can read which is most gratifying.' . . . [T]hese new-born children of freedom were not forgotten; and in October of the same year, . . . organized work was begun among them."

She tells us that, in a letter to the American Missionary Association, the Rev. Lockwood appealed at once for " 'primers, and for two or three female teachers to open week-day schools.' . . . A little later in the year, he writes that 'on November 17, the first day-school was opened with twenty scholars and a colored teacher, Mrs. Peake, who, before the war, being free herself, had privately instructed many of her people who were still enslaved, although such work was not without its dangers.' " Instructing children in the morning and adults in the evening, Mary Peake taught slave and free alike.

In December 1861, at the annual meeting of the American Missionary Association, it was resolved that "the new field of missionary labor in Virginia should be faithfully cultivated. . . ." And in January of the same year, in response to favorable progress reports highlighting the eagerness of the students to learn, the American Missionary Association sent a second wave of missionaries and teachers to assist the freedmen.

At a meeting at Cooper Institute in New York City on February 20, 1862, a committee having organized themselves as the National Freedmen's Relief Association announced a desire to work cooperatively with the federal government for the relief and improvement of the freedmen.

During the summer of 1862, General Samuel C. Armstrong was completing his studies at Williams College in Williamstown, Massachusetts. Upon graduation, he immediately entered the army as a captain in a New York regiment and shortly thereafter received a commission and a command in the U.S. Colored Troops. As the war went on, "refugees" or "freedmen," as they were increasingly referred to, continued to gather behind the Union lines at Fortress Freedom, among them, Robert Ellett, a former slave born in 1849.

> *. . . I came down to Hampton with my mother in June of 1863 as a refugee. Father was cooking for the Union Army and brother was waiting on a Colonel in General Storeman's Calvary. You see it happened this way. At the time McClelland [sic] was on the Pamuky River near White House Landing, Virginia, around Lee's farm. That was in 1862. Longstreet got behind McClelland and blowed up his magazine at White House Landing. The result was a Seven Day Battle. Then McClelland fell down to Harrison's landing and retreated by way of the Potomac River from Old Point Comfort. General Dicks made a raid around Fredericksburg and brought back . . . all the colored men to put them behind the Union lines where they could help fortify the place, cook food, and work for the officers. I saw the battle of the* Merrimac *and the* Monitor. *The shores was lined thick with people watching that strange fight.*

When the War Department officially began accepting African-American recruits, a total of 180,000 enlisted in the Union army. Among them was Lewis H. Harrison (Hampton Class of 1871), who served under Armstrong's command as a member of the Twenty-ninth U.S. Colored Troops. The First and Second U.S. Colored Cavalry and Battery B, Second Colored Light Artillery, were organized at Fortress Monroe. Nine other black regiments, organized elsewhere, also served in the theater of operations. After a day's battle, African-American troops often gathered around the fire at night to learn to read and write.

Mary S. Peake
(Courtesy of Casemate Museum, Hampton, Virginia)

According to many slave codes, educating slaves, which included teaching them to read, was a crime subject to severe punishment. As a result, most slaves found themselves illiterate and uneducated in a society where education was greatly valued and educated people highly esteemed. Although long denied its benefits, slaves understood the importance of education as an instrument of self-determination. Perhaps they also valued it as a means of regaining the dignity and respect stripped from them during their bondage.

Despite extreme poverty and great physical discomfort, these former slaves immediately attempted to rid themselves of ignorance as a badge of their former bondage. Endeavoring to elevate themselves above their circumstances, they exemplified the old African-American axiom "each one teach one" as they began the task of educating themselves. In cellars, private homes and, eventually, beneath the famous "Emancipation Oak," under which President Lincoln came to deliver the historic proclamation, they embarked on teaching one another.

In the town of Hampton, for example, the aged former slave of ex-president Tyler, who remained in charge of the president's property, established a primary school in the cellar of the Tyler mansion. Here he could be found seated with twenty-five "contraband" children standing at his knee as they worked to learn the alphabet. Holding up before them a well-worn spelling book, he would bow over it, turning it so that he could see the letters himself, and then pointing with his finger as he found his place, he would announce, "That's 'A'."

Mary Peake continued in her efforts to educate freedmen, giving to this great cause her "last full measure." Her early efforts are said to have marked the actual beginning of an organized movement to educate freedmen openly.

The Emancipation Oak
(Photograph by Jeff Krueger ©2000)

Peake, whose name is still cherished on the Hampton Peninsula, in effect launched the Virginia Freedmen's Education Program in 1861 when she began meeting with small groups of students. Within a few days her school had grown to fifty pupils. The educated daughter of a free colored woman and an Englishman, she was born Mary Smith Kelsey in Norfolk in 1823 and privately educated in Alexandria at a school for free blacks. In 1846 she returned to Hampton with her mother and stepfather, Thompson Walker, and although it was against the law, she began teaching slaves.

In 1851 she married Thomas Peake, a former slave who had been freed by a provision in his master's will. He served in the Mexican war and at sea until he settled down with Mary. During the Civil War, he served as a Union spy. The couple had one child, Daisy.

It is said that Mary Peake taught the first class of contraband children under the great live oak now

General Samuel C. Armstrong
(Courtesy of Casemate Museum, Hampton, Virginia)

known as the "Emancipation Oak." Peake was a highly spiritual woman, and her teachings included a strong religious emphasis. After the town of Hampton was burned by the Confederates on August 7, 1861, her family moved into the old Brown Cottage in Kecoughtan across the Hampton Creek, the place Mary Peake taught children in the mornings and grown-ups every afternoon. In her "spare" time, she helped organize classes in Newport News, Old Point, and Hampton. Although her health was rapidly failing she persisted, even on her deathbed, both in teaching and in religious exhortation. On Saturday, February 22, 1862, she died of tuberculosis at the age of thirty-nine.

The spirit of Mary Peake shone as a beacon before those eagerly seeking literacy as a first step toward equal citizenship. Mary Frances Armstrong notes that "After the president's proclamation . . . the demand for schools steadily increased. . . . [T]he number of [refugees] grew from month to month and the primary schools increased in number and capacity, one of them alone receiving within three months more than eight hundred scholars, while night-schools and Sunday-schools took in many who for various reasons could not attend during the usual day-school hours. . . . The Society of Friends of the North . . . sent several teachers to Hampton and the vicinity. . . . These teachers worked in hearty cooperation[,] [struggling] bravely with the gigantic undertaking, for the work, at this point, where there were not less than 1600 pupils, was growing so rapidly that failure here was especially to be dreaded.

"But no teachers of another race could do for the freed people what was waiting to be done by men and women of their own blood," Armstrong adds. In 1866, the American Missionary Association decided to open a normal school, and in January 1867 there appeared in *American Missionary Magazine* an article by General S. C. Armstrong, "earnestly and ably setting forth the need of normal schools for colored people, wherein they could be trained as teachers, and fitted to take up the work. . . ."

A Great Educational Work

Mary Frances Armstrong tells us that "At General's suggestion, the American Missionary Association purchased the 125 acre estate of 'Little Scotland' on Hampton Creek and converted the Government hospital there into a temporary school. Classes began in April of 1868 with General Armstrong as the principal, two teachers to assist him, and fifteen ex-slaves as pupils. General Armstrong saw that the need of the freedmen, now that their escape from slavery had become a certainty, was a training which should as swiftly as possible redeem their past and fit them for the demands that a near future was to make upon them."

Lizzie Gibbon's Story

"I was born a slave in the year 1852. I spent my happiest days of slavery in my childish days, and thought it was always to be just that way; but at the age of seven years that thought was changed, and a sorrowful change it was. I was then taken from my mother, as all the rest of the children [were]. My master, as I called him died, and being greatly in debt, we were first hired out to get money to pay the debts. This was not so grievous at first. We would get together and talk to each other about it and how we were going to eat good things when we got to our new homes; but just a few days before the hiring took place, I was struck to my heart with a scene I can never forget, and it was this. There was a very public place where I then lived, and all that wanted to hire, sell, or buy, would come here, generally in court week, or on the first day of the year. The streets would be crowded . . . and in the crowded street, sitting on the ground, was a colored woman with her children; her husband was standing a little way off from her crying. There walked up to him a white man, and said, 'Have you any clothes? If you have, get them.

You belong to me now. . . . Be quick about it, for I want to be off.' Then with a loud cry, the colored man said, 'I have nothing but my wife and children. Have you bought them too?' . . . 'No . . . I have bought none but you.' Then he begged to stay and see what was going to be done with his wife and his children, but the man screamed at him to get in the wagon to go, but would not tell him where he was going. Just at that time stepped up a very nice looking man who said, 'I have bought your wife and your baby, but the little boy I didn't get.' . . .

"... I stood and looked some time without stirring, and when I found myself the briny tears were trickling down my cheeks. This was my first dread of slavery. Then the day came for me to stand on the block . . . my sisters and brothers were scattered so that I never saw them again until we were called to this place again, not for the same light occasion, but it was for the fearful one of being sold.

"The war came and went . . . [t]hen came in the Emancipation, which was welcomed by every colored person, for it was the first time they were able to say, 'Glory to God in the highest, peace on earth, good-will to men' without being afraid. I could hear first one and then the other saying, 'I am free!'

"In October 1872, I came to Hampton and will still look to God for the future."

—Lizzie Gibbon, Hampton Class of 1875

It was in the inspired spirit of self-help that Hampton Institute was founded, not far from where the first Africans had landed in 1619, and on the very site where they had held a three-day prayer vigil for the Union's success and witnessed the battle of the *Monitor* and the *Merrimac*. How fitting that the school should be built on the site where "contraband" fought side by side with Union soldiers until victory was won, where they first heard the Emancipation Proclamation's sweet promise of self-determination, and implicit to it the right to education. It was upon this rock that Hampton Institute was founded and built.

A Beautiful Place for a School

"Just at the mouth of the Chesapeake Bay, where one of its numerous tributary creeks opens into the broad harbor of Hampton Roads, stands a little village, scattered along the western shore of the creek, with its half-ruined houses and low, white cabins irregularly clustered upon the level green meadows down to the very water's edge. . . . The back country through which the creek wanders for the few miles of its course, and the shore itself, are flat and monotonous, except for the brilliant coloring and golden, semi-tropical sunshine which for eight months in the year redeem the landscape from the latter charge. . . .

"But the changeful beauty of the shore, even when at its climax in the fresh spring months, can bear no comparison with the eternal beauty of the sea. . . . The sea, stretching far on either hand, offers by day and night, in calm and storm, new glories and beautiful, strange surprises of color and sound and motion. . . . When the fury of an Atlantic storm drives vessel after vessel into the secure anchorage of the roads, until a whole fleet is gathered under the guns of Old Point Comfort; or when on some breezy morning, scores of white-winged oyster-boats . . . put out from every nook of the shore, dotting the sparkling blue of the bay like snowy birds; or better. . . . When the fading crimson glow of sunset makes the [Hampton] shore shadowy and indistinct, . . . then one gazes and listens, to confess at last that such scenes are hard to rival."

—Mary Francis Armstrong, 1894

Such is the unrivaled beauty of Hampton, future home of the school by the sea! " '. . . Here,' General Armstrong . . . proclaim[ed], '[t]his is a beautiful spot for a school. See that knoll over there?' ([T]here was a knoll or bluff by the creek where Academic Hall now stands, with a salt marsh between it and the Mansion House.) 'It was on a slight rise, called Church Hill, that just eight years earlier, in 1862, escaped slaves, known as contraband, gathered by the thousands to watch the fight between the *Merrimac* and the *Monitor*. . . .' "

—Albert Howe, *Daily Press Newport,* March 19, 1925

xxvi A TASTE OF FREEDOM

Building a Team Brick by Brick

A large part of Hampton's growth was due to the forceful personality of General Samuel C. Armstrong, the school's indomitable chief, who gave his lifeblood in its service. Not only was he the team leader, he was a mentor and concerned friend to those who shared his vision and helped build the dream.

"... There was one thing about ... General Armstrong I thought very strange. Without a cent to begin with he would say, 'I want a house put here, we want it; we must have it'; but [while] digging out the foundation for it, I wondered how he would build that house.

"... I began work here in 1868. General Armstrong said, 'We are going to build a house over there.' He did not talk like other men who want to do anything and do not have the money to do it with. ... General Armstrong said, 'We cannot pay you but one dollar a week until you make one kiln of bricks.' Well, I thought it a pretty hard thing; still I did not say so. ... It took a long time to get the first kiln of brick made at Hampton. We started somewhere near the sawmill and the clay broke so badly that we could not finish the kiln with that clay so we moved. ...

"We went to work ... [and] worked away at one dollar per week until near the last of July when we made one kiln of brick, as [General Armstrong] said we would get the money then to pay for them. ... To finish the brick kiln, we went to where the shoe shop now is and molded enough clay to finish one kiln, we burned it, and a happier man you never saw than General Armstrong. ...

"When Hampton's brick kiln was finally finished, I was happy too, but [the General's and my] happiness was not just alike. He was happy because he had got a kiln of good bricks to start the Academic [and] I was happy I was going to get the other five dollars or more due per week. ... Anyhow there were two happy souls, General Armstrong and myself. ... But when I lost my leg and, was down and could not help myself [General Armstrong] ... took his own money and brought me wood and coal for two winters. ...

"I am crippled for life as you know, but I will do all I can to help. ... I helped make bricks for every brick building on the school grounds but three."

—Edward Jones, Hampton employee, 1894

Brick kiln in which bricks for Virginia Hall were burned
(Reproduced from the collections of the Library of Congress)

Building a Dream

Early Hampton pioneers taught, while others raised money. Still others set about the task of building a legacy from the ground up. Among them was Albert Howe, a Civil War veteran and store owner who enjoyed the distinction of sharing in the vision and the labor of General Armstrong from the very beginning.

" '. . . That's just the place for an academic building,' he said. . . . That will be the spot for the Academic Hall and just here for a building for girls and a general dining-room. We'll call it Virginia Hall.' He gave it the very name it bears now. . . . Then [General Armstrong] pointed out sites for boy's cottages—all as you see it now. I sat on a log and just looked at him and laughed. I thought he was a visionary. It all came to pass. Nothing was impossible to him—not a thing. . . . [General Armstrong] sat there and talked in that dreamy voice. . . . I thought he was a visionary, and he did see visions; he was inspired. He pictured out just about what we see now, the industries, farms, shops and all. . . .

"After Academic Hall was begun, we at last had no more money to pay hands. 'How much money do we owe on this building?' said . . . General [Armstrong] to me. The bricks were all made. We footed up all the bills and found we owed $17,000. 'Well,' said the General, 'I'm going North.' . . . He went to General Howard and to Mrs. Hemenway— and the money came as it always did. . . .

"Then came Virginia Hall. There wasn't $2000.00 in sight for it when it was begun. It cost $70,000.00. . . . According to Howe, 'the way to do is to plough out a hole and pile the bricks and lumber around. [Get] a party of people down from the North and make it appeal to them.' So he did. . . . The basement was commenced so they could see the work underway. A large party came down, some of the best people of New York and Boston. . . . The tide was way up when they landed; the ladies had to come sliding down the gang plank. Miss Lottie prepared refreshments—ice cream and strawberries and crab salad. . . . We had a grand time and the money came. . . ."

—Albert Howe, *Daily Press Newport,* March 19, 1925

BEVERAGES

"Miss Tyler used to make coffee in her apartment by various scientific processes of distillation, while she gave drawing lessons, superintended galvanic batteries, carved cameos and ate nuts and apples all at one and the same moment, her admiring friends and co-workers sitting awe-struck about the room on trunks, beds and chairs, while this marvelous woman carried on simultaneously her cooking, her teaching, her carving, her electrical experimenting, and a steady flow of informing and interesting conversation."

—Alice M. Bacon, Hampton student, 1894

Pink Lavender Lemonade

5	cups water, divided		2¼	cups fresh lemon juice
2½	cups superfine sugar		2	tablespoons grenadine syrup
12	fresh lavender stems (unsprayed, pesticide-free)		1–2	drops red food coloring (optional) Lavender blossoms
3	tablespoons dried pink hibiscus flowers (unsprayed, pesticide-free)			

Bring 2½ cups of the water and the sugar to a boil. Add the lavender stems and dried hibiscus flowers and remove from the heat. Cover and allow to cool at room temperature. When cool, remove the lavender stems. Add the lemon juice, grenadine, and food coloring and remaining water, if desired, and mix well. Strain through a sieve into a serving pitcher. Pour into tall glasses filled with crushed ice. Garnish with lavender blossoms.

6 to 8 servings

Strawberry Rhubarb Lemon-Limeade

4½	cups water		2	cups strawberries, hulled and sliced
½	pound rhubarb, trimmed and cut into 1-inch pieces (stalks only)		½	cup fresh lemon juice
¾	cup sugar, or to taste		½	cup fresh lime juice Whole ripe strawberries, for garnish

In a large saucepan combine the water, rhubarb pieces, and sugar; bring to a rolling boil and stir until the sugar is completely dissolved. Reduce to a simmer; cover and continue to simmer over low heat for an additional 10 minutes. Add the strawberries and stir. Bring the mixture to a second boil and reduce to a simmer. Cover and simmer for an additional 2 minutes. Remove the saucepan from the heat and allow the mixture to completely cool before straining through a sieve set over a pitcher. Press hard on the solids to remove all liquids. Stir in the lemon and lime juices and mix well. Adjust the flavor to taste by adding additional water and/or sugar. Pour the lemonade into tall, ice-filled, frosted glasses and garnish with a whole strawberry. To frost glasses, set them on a tray in the freezer compartment until covered with frost. Dip the rims in sugar and fill with beverage, or return unfilled glasses to the freezer for the sugar to set properly.

4 to 6 servings

Fortress Monroe, Ocean View
"Just at the mouth of the Chesapeake Bay, where one of its numerous tributary creeks opens into the broad harbor of Hampton Roads, stands a little village, scattered along the western shore of the creek, with its half-ruined houses and low, white cabins irregularly clustered upon the level green meadows down to the very water's edge. . . ." —Mary Frances Armstrong *(Reproduced from the collections of the Library of Congress)*

The Brave Struggle

". . . So, in the midst uncertainties, [and] with no sure promise of support, the school began its life and inaugurated its work in April, 1868, . . . with twenty scholars and two academic teachers. . . . The treasury was sometimes absolutely empty, and the coming of the next dollar an entire uncertainty, yet, in obedience to some unknown law of supply and demand, the next dollar never failed to come and save [Hampton] from a bankruptcy which was more than once threatened.

". . . Incorporated by the General Assembly of Virginia, in June 1870, as the Hampton Normal and Agricultural Institute, students began flocking to the school as its educational plan became more generally understood. . . . As enrollment increased, the number of teachers was necessarily increased and a home was furnished for them in one of the houses purchased with the farm . . . while a long line of deserted barracks and a second building, formerly used as a grist-mill, were taken for girls' dormitories."

—Mary Frances Armstrong

OLD-FASHIONED HONEY LEMONADE

1¼   cups fresh lemon juice   1¼   cups hot water
1   cup honey   3¼   cups cold water

In a heatproof container, combine the lemon juice, honey, and hot water. Stir until thoroughly mixed. Adjust the flavor to your taste by adding additional honey or water, if desired. Transfer to a serving container and add cold water. Mix well and chill. Serve in tall, ice-filled, frosted glasses. Garnish with fresh lemon slices. To frost glasses, set them on a tray in the freezer compartment until covered with frost. Dip the rims in sugar and fill with beverage, or return unfilled glasses to the freezer for the sugar to set properly.

4 to 6 servings

BLACKBERRY LEMONADE

2½   pints fresh blackberries *or*   1½   cups fresh lemon juice
    1 16-ounce package frozen   1½   cups sugar
    unsweetened blackberries,   3   cups hot water
    thawed   5   cups cold water

Purée the berries and transfer the purée to a sieve set over a heatproof serving pitcher. Gently press the berry juice through the sieve with the back of a spoon. Discard the pulp. In a heatproof container, mix the strained blackberry juice with the lemon juice, sugar, and hot water. Stir until the sugar dissolves. Add the cold water and additional sugar to taste; refrigerate to chill. Serve with fresh mint sprigs and/or lemon slices.

6 to 8 servings

GINGER LEMONADE

4½ cups water, divided
¾ cup sugar
2½ tablespoons minced fresh
    gingerroot

1 cup fresh lemon juice
¼ cup fresh lime juice

In a medium saucepan, combine 2¼ cups of the water with the sugar and gingerroot. Bring to a boil and stir until the sugar dissolves. Reduce to a simmer; cover and continue to simmer for an additional 5 minutes. Strain the mixture through a fine sieve set over a bowl and allow to cool before transferring to a serving pitcher. Add the remaining 2¼ cups water and remaining ingredients. Stir well; pour into tall, ice-filled, frosted glasses. To frost glasses, set them on a tray in the freezer compartment until covered with frost. Dip the rims in sugar and fill with beverage, or return unfilled glasses to the freezer for the sugar to set properly.

4 to 6 servings

APRICOT NECTAR

3 12-ounce cans apricot nectar
⅓ cup sugar

½ cup fresh lemon juice
1 quart carbonated lemon-lime soda

Combine the first three ingredients in a 2-quart serving pitcher. Mix well until the sugar dissolves and refrigerate to chill. Just before serving, add the carbonated lemon soda. Stir well and pour into tall, ice-filled glasses.

4 to 6 servings

Mansion House, Old Memorial Church and Academic Hall
" '. . . Here,' General Armstrong . . . proclaim[ed], . . . 'is a beautiful spot for a school. See that knoll over there?' There was a knoll or bluff by the creek where Academic Hall now stands, with a salt marsh between it and the Mansion House. It was on a slight rise, called Church Hill, where just eight years earlier, in 1862, escaped slaves, known as contraband, gathered by the thousands to watch the fight between the *Merrimac* and the *Monitor*. . . ." —Albert Howe, *Daily Press Newport,* March 19, 1925 *(Reproduced from the collections of the Library of Congress)*

PEACH NECTAR AND BASIL LEMONADE

There is nothing quite as refreshing as a cold drink on a hot summer day. These recipes hearken back to an earlier time when the offer of a cool drink brought welcome respite from summer heat as well as an opportunity to socialize. This refreshing lemonade is among my favorites.

2 cups water	½ cup fresh lemon juice
1 cup fresh basil leaves	Spearmint or basil sprigs, for
½ cup sugar, or to taste	garnish
3 12-ounce cans apricot nectar	

In a medium saucepan, combine the water, basil, and sugar; bring the mixture to a boil, stirring until the sugar dissolves. Reduce the heat and simmer for an additional 5 minutes. Allow the mixture to cool before straining through a fine sieve set over a serving pitcher. Discard the basil from the strainer. Stir in the remaining ingredients and pour into tall, ice-filled, frosted glasses. Garnish with a sprig of fresh spearmint or basil. To frost glasses, set them on a tray in the freezer compartment until covered with frost. Dip the rims in sugar and fill with beverage, or return unfilled glasses to the freezer for the sugar to set properly.

4 servings

ICED TEA NECTAR

8 cups boiling water	18 ounces unsweetened pineapple juice
8 tea bags	24 ounces apricot juice
1-inch cinnamon stick	2½ cups cold water
1 cup sugar	Garnish of choice

In a large pitcher, pour the boiling water over the tea bags and cinnamon stick; steep for 5 minutes. Remove and discard the tea bags; add the sugar and stir until it dissolves. Remove the cinnamon stick and discard. Refrigerate the tea to cool. Before serving, add the remaining ingredients; mix well, transfer to a serving pitcher, and pour into ice-filled glasses. Garnish with fresh pineapple, lime, or lemon slices, and a sprig of fresh spearmint.

8 servings

SPARKLING RASPBERRY TEA

1 pint fresh raspberries	Lemon quarters, for garnish
4 cups warm tea	Cloves, for garnish
1 cup sugar	Fresh spearmint sprigs, for garnish
2½ tablespoons fresh lemon juice	
2 12-ounce cans carbonated lemon-lime soda	

Rinse the raspberries and set aside to drain. Combine the next three ingredients in a large pitcher and stir until the sugar dissolves. Next, purée the berries (or place them in a large bowl and mash with a potato masher until they are reduced to a pulp). Transfer the purée to a sieve placed over the pitcher and use the back of a spoon to press the juice from the berries into the pitcher. Discard the pulp; stir well and refrigerate. Stud lemon quarters with cloves and set aside. Before serving, add lemon-lime soda. Garnish glasses with clove-studded lemon quarters and a sprig of fresh spearmint.

4 to 6 servings

CITRUS TEA

I love a bright summer day, especially on the coast, where bright whites, pastoral blues, and lemon yellow provide a tropical blend. This citrus tea is just the right blend for those sunny summer days. One sip and you will think that you are in the tropics.

5	English Breakfast tea bags		¼	cup fresh lemon juice
2	orange pekoe tea bags		¼	cup fresh lime juice
5	fresh mint leaves		⅓	cup sugar, or to taste
8	cups boiling water		4	cups cold water
¼	cup fresh orange juice			Mint leaves, for garnish

In a heatproof pitcher or bowl, combine the first four ingredients, stir well, and steep for 10 minutes. Discard the tea bags and mint leaves. Chill and add the remaining ingredients. Stir well. Adjust the flavor to taste by adding additional water and/or sugar. Pour into tall, ice-filled glasses. Garnish with mint leaves.

8 to 10 servings

RED RASPBERRY SHRUB

1	quart red raspberries		¾	cup sugar
1	quart water		½	cup lemon juice

Purée the berries or place them in a large bowl and mash with a potato masher until they are reduced to a pulp. Bring the water to a boil, add the sugar and lemon juice, and continue to boil until the sugar dissolves. Pour the hot mixture over the berries. Allow the mixture to cool, then press it through a large sieve; press the solids hard against the side until all liquid is removed. Discard the mash. Transfer the liquid to a serving pitcher and refrigerate. Pour into tall glasses filled with crushed ice.

8 to 10 servings

Raspberry Champagne Cocktail

1 pint fresh raspberries
2 tablespoons superfine sugar
½ cup plus 2 tablespoons
   raspberry liqueur
¼ cup cognac
8 sugar cubes

Cointreau
1 750-milliliter bottle chilled brut
   champagne
Fresh raspberries, for garnish
Lemon peel strips, for garnish

Combine the raspberries and sugar in a medium bowl. Mash the berries lightly with a fork. Allow to stand undisturbed for 15 minutes. Stir in the cognac and raspberry liqueur. Pour into a jar; cover tightly with a lid and let stand in a dark cupboard for at least 3 days, but up to 1 month. Before serving, strain the liquid and set aside; discard the mash. Dip the sugar cubes in Cointreau. Place 1 cube in each of eight 6-ounce champagne flutes. Pour 2 tablespoons of raspberry mixture over the sugar cube. Fill each glass with champagne and garnish with raspberries and lemon strips.

6 servings

APPETIZERS

"Life at Hampton was a constant revelation to me . . . constantly taking me into a new world. The matter of having meals at regular hours, of eating on a tablecloth, using a napkin . . . were all new to me."

—Booker T. Washington

Growth and Expansion

"In 1871 the boys, . . . roomed in the upper story of the first Academic Hall, eight or ten to a room. Even the library, or large room that was used for a library was turned into a bedroom at night."

—George J. Davis, Hampton, Class of 1874

Unaware of Hampton's crowded conditions and unlikely to be deterred even if they knew, the students kept coming. . . . "Soon General Armstrong got hold of six or eight army tents and set them in a line between Academic and the shore, about where Mrs. Armstrong's cottage is now. . . ."

—George J. Davis, Hampton, Class of 1874

". . . Our little student camp is pitched for its second winter, and cheerfully filled with those who know how to endure hardness as good soldiers in the struggle for education. Our girls, too, ought not to be left out in this testimony to their people's hunger and thirst after knowledge. Till Virginia Hall is finished, they are exhibiting an equal patience and courage in their dark and crowded barracks almost as shelterless as the tents. . . ."

—Mary Frances Armstrong, Hampton teacher, 1894

". . . As soon as it became known that General Armstrong would be pleased if some of the older students would live in the tents during the winter, nearly every student volunteered to go. . . ." I was one of the volunteers. The winter that we spent in those tents was an intensely cold one and we suffered severely—how much I am sure General Armstrong never knew, because we made no complaints. . . . More than once during the cold night, when a still gale would be blowing, our tent was lifted bodily, and we would find ourselves in the open air. . . . It was enough for us to know that we were pleasing General Armstrong, and that we were making it possible for an additional number of students to secure an education. . . ."

—Booker T. Washington, Hampton, Class of 1875

Pressmen at work in the Hampton printing shop

"The printing-office connected with the school was founded by the gift of one thousand dollars from Mrs. Augustus Hemenway, of Boston, and was open for business November 1st, 1871, beginning with two small presses. . . . These generous gifts have greatly increased the working facilities in the office, which is the only one in Hampton. [Those] employed in the office are selected as showing particular aptitude for the business, and the majority of them make rapid progress—one indeed having been able to during the past year to pay his way in school by work done out of school hours." —Mary Frances Armstrong *(Reproduced from the collections of the Library of Congress)*

BAKED VIRGINIA CRAB CAKES

Mary Frances Armstrong

2	pounds backfin crabmeat	⅓	cup mayonnaise
¾	cup soft white bread crumbs	1	tablespoon prepared mustard
2	tablespoons minced onion	2	teaspoons Worcestershire sauce
2	teaspoons Old Bay Seafood Seasoning (see page 110)	1	teaspoon hot pepper sauce
		2	tablespoons melted butter
½	teaspoon black pepper		Paprika

Preheat the oven to 400 degrees F. Lightly grease a baking sheet and set it aside. In a bowl, gently flake the crabmeat, removing any cartilage, and refrigerate while preparing the remaining ingredients. Mix the bread, onion, and seasonings in a bowl. Gently fold in the crabmeat. Blend the mayonnaise, mustard, Worcestershire, and hot pepper sauce in a separate small bowl. Gently fold this into the crab mixture, combining until well blended. Divide equally and shape into eight cakes. Arrange on the prepared sheet. Sprinkle with paprika. Brush with melted butter and bake until lightly browned, approximately 10 to 12 minutes.

4 to 8 servings

CORN-BREAD-FRIED OYSTERS

You will experience the unique flavor of southern seafood when you taste one of these delicious oysters fried with a tasty cornbread batter. One bite and you will never return to traditional flour batters.

1½	cups yellow cornmeal	2	cups half-and-half
½	cup all-purpose flour	1	tablespoon baking powder
2	tablespoons Paul Prudhomme's seafood seasoning	¼	cup bacon drippings
		3	cups vegetable oil
¼	teaspoon salt	36	freshly shucked oysters
½	teaspoon cayenne pepper		Lime wedges, for garnish
2	eggs, lightly beaten		

In a medium bowl, combine the first nine ingredients. Stir the batter until smooth. In a deep-fat fryer or large kettle, heat the vegetable oil. Dredge each oyster in the cornmeal batter and fry in batches until golden brown, about 1 minute. Remove with a slotted spoon, drain on a paper towel, and serve immediately with lime wedges.

4 to 6 servings

ANGELS ON HORSEBACK

1	teaspoon seasoned salt	Pinch of cayenne pepper
½	teaspoon onion powder	2 pints select oysters
¼	teaspoon black pepper	1 pound hickory smoked bacon
⅛	teaspoon paprika	

Preheat the oven to 450 degrees F. Combine the seasonings and sprinkle over the oysters. Fry the bacon until limp and transparent but not crisp. Wrap each oyster with half a strip of bacon; secure with a toothpick, and place on a rack in a shallow baking pan. Bake for 10 to 12 minutes or until the bacon is crisp. Serve on melba toast rounds.

4 to 6 servings

SHRIMP BOILED IN BEER

3	pounds medium shrimp	3 bay leaves
36	ounces beer	4 teaspoons Tabasco sauce
4	garlic cloves, peeled and crushed	1½ teaspoons celery seeds
1	tablespoon Old Bay Seafood Seasoning (see page 110)	1 teaspoon cayenne pepper
		Juice of ½ lemon
		Unsalted butter, for serving

Wash the shrimp, but do not remove the shells. Combine the remaining ingredients and bring to a boil in a large pot. Add the shrimp, bring to a second boil, reduce the heat to low, and simmer, uncovered, until the shrimp are pink, approximately 2 to 5 minutes. Drain and serve with plenty of melted, unsalted butter seasoned with more lemon juice, Old Bay Seasoning to taste, and Tabasco.

6 to 8 servings

BROILED SHRIMP

3	pounds medium shrimp	1½	teaspoons Worcestershire sauce
4	garlic cloves, minced	1	teaspoon paprika
5	shallots, minced	½	teaspoon garlic powder
1	cup (2 sticks) butter, melted	¼	teaspoon onion powder
2	tablespoons vegetable oil		Seasoned salt and black pepper
	Juice of 1 lime		to taste

Wash the shrimp; drain and set aside. Combine the shrimp with all remaining ingredients except the salt and pepper. Refrigerate for about an hour. Place in a single layer in a shallow baking pan with the butter sauce. Lightly sprinkle with seasoned salt and pepper to taste, then broil for 12 to 15 minutes, or until the shrimp turn pink and opaque and their tails are slightly curled. Serve hot.

6 to 8 servings

CAROLYN'S SPICY BBQ SHRIMP

3	pounds medium shrimp, peeled, boiled, and deveined	2	tablespoons lemon juice
		¼	teaspoon onion powder
2	cups prepared barbecue sauce	⅛	teaspoon garlic powder
2	tablespoons vegetable oil	¼	teaspoon paprika
¼	cup hot pepper sauce	¼	teaspoon cayenne pepper
		½	teaspoon seasoned salt

Preheat the oven to 350 degrees F. Wash the shrimp. Bring enough water to cook the shrimp to a rapid boil. Immerse the shrimp in the boiling water for 1 to 2 minutes. Promptly transfer the shrimp to a colander and rinse under very cold water. Set aside and allow the shrimp to completely drain. Combine the shrimp and the remaining ingredients; place in a single layer on a shallow baking pan and bake for 10 to 12 minutes. Serve hot.

6 to 8 servings

General O. O. Howard, head of the Freedmen's Bureau, c. 1900
(Reproduced from the collections of the Library of Congress)

CAVIAR DIP

½ cup whipping cream
¼ cup red caviar
2 tablespoons chopped shallots

3 hard-boiled eggs, chopped
¼ cup finely chopped chives

Whip the cream, then fold in the caviar and chopped shallots. Mix gently. Place in a serving bowl and garnish the outer edges with chopped eggs and chives. Serve with small rounds of toast.

Yields approximately 1 cup

CLAM DIP

2 8-ounce cans chopped clams
8 ounces soft cream cheese
¾ cup dairy sour cream
1½ teaspoons chopped chives

½ teaspoon salt
¼ teaspoon cracked black pepper
¼ teaspoon garlic powder
1 teaspoon Tabasco sauce

Drain and reserve the juice from the clams. Place the clam juice, cream cheese, and sour cream in a processor. Process with a steel blade until smooth. In a bowl, combine the clam mixture and the remaining ingredients. Use clam juice to adjust the dip's consistency to taste. Either discard the remaining juice or freeze it for future use. Serve chilled.

Yields approximately 2½ cups

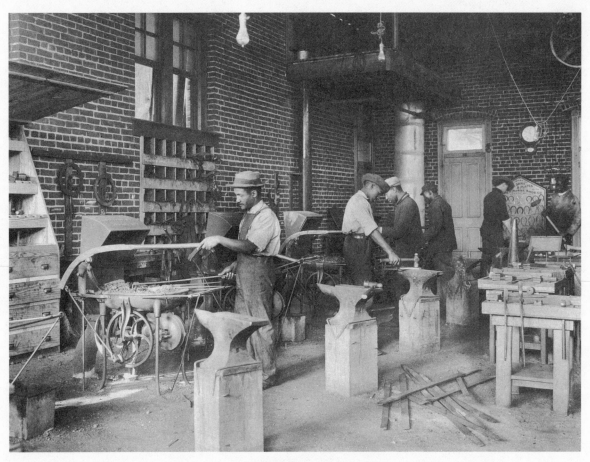

Blacksmith shop
"These different departments of manual labor furnish such variety of instruction as admirably pre-
pares the students for the uncertainty of their futures lives, and [at the] end of the three year's course[,]
to choose between several occupations, in any one of which they can serve with honor and profit to
themselves." —Mary Frances Armstrong, Hampton teacher, 1894 *(Reproduced from the collections of
the Library of Congress)*

GRILLED SCALLOPS AND SHRIMP WITH BACON

8	lean bacon slices	1	pound large shrimp
1	pound large sea scallops		

Blanch the bacon in boiling water for about 3 minutes to remove some of the fat and to partially cook the bacon. Using either metal skewers or wooden skewers that have been soaked in water, pierce one end of a bacon strip, then skewer a scallop. Loop the bacon over the top and skewer. Skewer a shrimp, loop the bacon over the top, and skewer. Repeat this process until each skewer is filled. Grill over a hot charcoal grill or under a broiler for approximately 8 to 10 minutes or until the shrimp are opaque and the bacon is crisp.

8 servings

STUFFED CRAB

Crab is, without a doubt, my favorite seafood. I love it boiled, fried, in salad, and combined with cornbread to make a great seafood stuffing for fish. This recipe for stuffed crab is a favorite among friends and family, who often request it.

4	large whole cooked crabs, cracked	3	large garlic cloves, chopped
1	pound lump crabmeat	2	teaspoons chopped jalapeño pepper
1	cup fresh white bread crumbs	¾	teaspoon cayenne pepper
½	cup milk	¼	teaspoon ground cloves
2	tablespoons vegetable oil		Pinch of ground nutmeg
1	cup chopped onion	⅛	teaspoon paprika
2	tablespoons chopped celery	3	tablespoons fresh lemon juice
¼	cup chopped chives	2	tablespoons fresh lime juice
			Salt and black pepper to taste

Preheat the oven to 350 degrees F. Remove the crabmeat from shells; rinse the shells and set aside to drain. Place the crabmeat in a bowl, add the bread and milk, and mix well. In a heavy medium saucepan, heat the oil over medium heat. Add the onion, celery, chives, garlic, jalapeño, and spices. Sauté until the onion is soft. Add the crabmeat mixture and cook for an additional 2 minutes. Remove the skillet from the heat; add the lemon and lime juices, and salt and pepper to taste. Spoon the mixture into the reserved shells. Bake for approximately 10 minutes, sprinkle with paprika, and then brown under the broiler.

4 servings

Students learning bricklaying
(Reproduced from the collections of the Library of Congress)

CRAB DELIGHT

1½   cups sour cream
¾   cup mayonnaise
1   pound backfin crabmeat
1   tablespoon grated onion
1½   tablespoons chopped chives

1½   tablespoons sherry
2   tablespoons lemon juice
     Salt and black pepper to taste
⅛   teaspoon paprika
     Pinch of cayenne pepper

Mix the above ingredients and chill for 2 hours before serving on toast rounds or crackers.

Yields approximately 3 cups

Dr. Howe's residence
(Reproduced from the collections of the Library of Congress)

GRILLED GARLIC-LIME WINGS

3 pounds chicken wings	⅓ cup olive oil
½ teaspoon garlic powder	¾ cup fresh lime juice
¼ teaspoon onion powder	Grated zest of 3 limes
¼ teaspoon cayenne pepper	7 garlic cloves, minced
2 teaspoons finely chopped garlic	Salt to taste

Wash the chicken wings and separate at the joints. Discard the tips or freeze for future use. In a large mixing bowl, combine the next four ingredients. Add the chicken to the bowl and rub the spices into it. Add the olive oil, lime juice, lime zest, and minced garlic. Refrigerate for 2 or 3 hours prior to cooking. Salt the chicken to taste, transfer it with tongs to an oiled grill set about 6 inches above glowing coals, and baste with the marinade during cooking. Grill for 12 to 15 minutes on each side or until the chicken is cooked through. (It can also be baked in a 450-degree F. oven for 30 to 35 minutes or until cooked through.) Cover with aluminum foil and keep warm until ready to serve.

6 to 8 servings

HERBED GARLIC WINGS

3 pounds chicken wings	2 teaspoons dried rosemary leaves
½ cup fresh lemon juice	½ teaspoon dried basil
¼ cup water	¼ teaspoon cayenne pepper
¼ cup olive oil	Grated zest of 2 lemons
½ teaspoon garlic powder	Salt to taste
5 garlic cloves, minced	

Marinate the chicken for anywhere from several hours to a day in advance. Wash the chicken wings and separate at the joints. Discard the tips or freeze for future use. In a large mixing bowl, combine the next nine ingredients, and salt to taste. Add the chicken to the bowl; toss to coat with marinade. Cover and refrigerate. To cook the wings, preheat the oven to 350 degrees F. Lightly oil two rimmed baking sheets. Arrange the wings on the baking sheets; drizzle with marinade. Bake the wings uncovered, turning once, until golden (approximately 30 minutes). Brush occasionally with marinade drippings from the baking sheet. Serve immediately.

12 servings

SPINACH DIP

2 rounds fresh sheepherder's bread (firm, round loaves available at most bakeries)	½ cup sliced green onions, including tops
	¼ cup freshly grated Parmesan cheese
	2 tablespoons lemon juice
10 ounces frozen chopped spinach, thawed	½ teaspoon seasoned salt
	½ ounce powdered ranch dressing mix
1 pint sour cream	⅛ teaspoon Tabasco sauce

Cut off the tops of the bread and scoop out the insides; retain the bread pieces and set aside. Next, combine all remaining ingredients except bread. Fill the bread with dip and serve with bread pieces and lavash (Armenian cracker bread).

8 to 12 servings

VEGETABLE DIP

1 cup mayonnaise	2 tablespoons lemon juice
1 pint sour cream	½ teaspoon seasoned salt
¼ cup freshly grated Parmesan cheese	½ ounce powdered ranch dressing mix
	½ teaspoon Tabasco sauce

Combine the above ingredients and mix well. Chill. Serve with vegetable crudités.

12 to 18 servings

Compositors at work in the printing shop
"[T]he neighborhood affords a fair regular supply of job-work, while an illustrated paper, the *Southern Workman,* is Published monthly, for circulation among the industrial classes of the south, among whom it has been met with a very favorable reception." —Mary Frances Armstrong, Hampton teacher, 1894 *(Reproduced from the collections of the Library of Congress)*

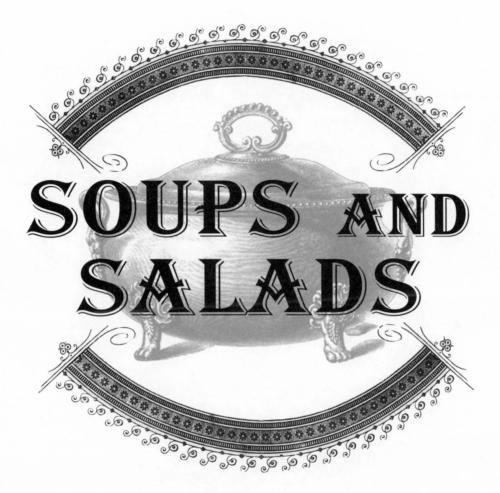

SOUPS AND SALADS

The warm fragrance of a simmering soup pot always reminds me of my mother's kitchen and the love that waited for me there on cold winter days.

—C.Q.T.

Fresh Asparagus Soup

2	pounds fresh asparagus	47	ounces chicken broth
3	tablespoons butter	2	egg yolks, beaten
⅓	cup sliced green onions, including green tops	¾	cup whipping cream Paprika, for garnish

Wash and trim the asparagus, removing and discarding any white fibrous ends. Remove the tips, then cut the remainder of the asparagus into 1-inch pieces.

In a large saucepan, melt the butter over medium heat. Add the green onions and sauté until limp, approximately 5 minutes. Set aside approximately half of your best tips. Add the remaining tips and asparagus to the onions and cook, covered, over medium-low heat for approximately 20 minutes or until the asparagus is very tender. Remove from the heat and set aside. In a separate pot, steam the reserved asparagus tips until tender, drain, and set aside. Purée the chicken broth and asparagus mixture until smooth. Return the soup to the pan and add the egg yolks and cream. Reheat the soup, but do not allow it to come to a boil. Garnish with steamed asparagus tips and a dash of paprika prior to serving.

6 servings

Great Northern Bean Soup

1	pound dried great northern beans	2	onions, chopped
4	cups water	1	bay leaf
4	cups chicken broth	2	garlic cloves, minced
1	ham hock	2½	cups diced ham
2	tablespoons bacon drippings		Salt and black pepper to taste

Place the beans in a large colander and remove stones or other foreign objects. Rinse the beans in cold water and then remove them to a large bowl. Add sufficient water to cover by 3 inches. Soak overnight. Drain. Place the water, broth, and washed ham hock in a large pot; bring to a quick boil. Reduce the heat to low and simmer the ham hock for 1 hour. Add the beans and additional liquid to cover. Bring to a quick boil over high heat. Reduce the heat to medium low and simmer for 1 hour. Add the onions, bay leaf, garlic, and chopped ham. Cover and simmer for an additional hour. Add water as necessary to let the beans boil freely and avoid scorching.

Season to taste with salt and pepper. Serve hot. For a creamier soup, remove the beans from the pot when tender, process through a food processor, then return the mixture to the pot and add the remaining ingredients.

6 servings

Hampton students in a chemistry class
(Reproduced from the collections of the Library of Congress)

Black Bean Soup
With Horseradish Cream

1	pound dried black beans		1¼	teaspoons seasoned salt
1	large yellow onion		1	tablespoon fresh lemon juice
2	green bell peppers		⅓	cup dry Madeira (available at most liquor stores)
4	garlic cloves, minced		⅛	teaspoon thyme
3	bay leaves			Horseradish Cream, for garnish (below)
¼	cup olive oil			
1	gallon water		½	cup chopped chives, for garnish
2	ham hocks			

Pick over the beans, removing any foreign objects. In a large bowl, soak the beans overnight in sufficient cold water to cover by 3 inches. The next day, in a heavy 3- to 4-quart pot, sauté the yellow onion, green peppers, garlic, and bay leaves in the olive oil over medium-low heat. Be careful not to burn the garlic. Add the water and ham hocks to the pot, bring to a rapid boil, and reduce the heat to low. Drain and rinse the beans, and add them to the pot. If necessary, add additional water to cover beans by 3 inches.

Add the seasoned salt, cover the pot, and cook over low heat for about an hour or until the beans are extremely tender and the liquid thickens. Remove and discard the tough outer skin from the ham hocks. Remove the meat from the bones and return it to the soup. Remove and discard the bay leaves. Purée the soup in a food processor or rub it through a fine sieve with the back of a spoon. Add the lemon juice, return the soup to the pot, and, stirring constantly, bring it to a simmer over moderate heat. Stir in the Madeira and thyme and serve. Garnish individual servings with a dollop of Horseradish Cream and chopped chives.

6 servings

Horseradish Cream

½	cup well-chilled whipping cream		2	teaspoons prepared horseradish
¾	teaspoon curry powder			Salt and black pepper to taste

In a chilled bowl, beat the cream until it holds soft peaks, then add the curry powder, horseradish, and salt and pepper. Beat again until stiff peaks begin to form. Use as a garnish for the hot soup.

Yields ½ cup

BLACK-EYED PEA SOUP

1 pound dried black-eyed peas
1 smoked ham hock
1 bay leaf
1 large onion, chopped
½ cup finely chopped celery
1 cup chicken broth

1½ pounds smoked ham, cubed
1 cup heavy whipping cream, for
     garnish
Paprika, for garnish
1 cup chopped green onions, for
     garnish

Place the peas in a large colander, and pick over to remove stones or other foreign objects. Rinse the beans in cold water and put them in a large bowl. Add sufficient water to cover by 3 inches. Soak overnight. Drain. Place the washed ham hock and water to cover in a 3- to 4-quart pot and bring to a quick boil. Reduce the heat to medium low and simmer the ham hock for 1 hour. Add the beans, onion, celery, and bay leaf with enough liquid to cover by at least 3 inches. Allow the peas to simmer for 1 hour. When the peas are done, discard the bay leaf. Remove the ham hock from the pot and let it cool. Remove the lean meat from ham hock. Place this meat, half of the peas, and the chicken broth in a blender and purée until smooth. Return the purée to the pot, and add the chopped ham. Purée the remaining peas and return those to the pot as well. Warm the soup over medium-low heat. When it's warmed through, ladle into individual serving dishes, garnishing with whipped cream, a sprinkle of paprika, and chopped green onions. Serve with corn bread.

6 servings

PINTO BEAN SOUP

1 pound dried pinto beans
¼ pound uncooked bacon,
     chopped
1 large yellow onion, chopped
1 cup diced green bell pepper
2 garlic cloves, minced

¼ pound kielbasa or other smoked
     sausage
Salt and black pepper to taste
½ teaspoon crushed red pepper
2 cups cooked white rice

Pick over the beans, removing any foreign objects. In a large bowl, soak the beans overnight in sufficient cold water to cover by 3 inches. The next day, sauté the bacon in a heavy 3- to 4-quart pot until transparent. Add the onion, green bell pepper, and garlic. Stirring constantly, sauté for 2 to 3 minutes until softened; remove from the heat. Drain and rinse the beans. Add drained beans and sausage to the pot with the bacon and vegetables and sufficient water to cover the ingredients by 3 inches. Bring the mixture to a rapid boil; reduce the heat to medium low, and simmer for 1½ to 2 hours, or until the beans are tender. Season with salt and pepper to taste, along with crushed pepper. Just prior to serving, stir in the rice.

6 servings

CATFISH STEW

5	lean bacon slices	3	tablespoons Worcestershire sauce
2	tablespoons coarsely chopped salt pork	1	teaspoon Tabasco sauce
1¾	cups finely chopped onion	1	teaspoon celery salt
¼	cup chopped green bell pepper	1	teaspoon salt
5	large, firm, ripe tomatoes, coarsely chopped	4	cups water
		½	teaspoon cayenne pepper
2	cups white potatoes, peeled and cut into 1-inch cubes	2	pounds catfish fillets, cut into 1½-inch pieces
1	pound catfish trimmings (head, tail, and bones of the fish)	4	cups cooked rice

In a heavy 4- to 6-quart casserole, fry the bacon until crisp, remove from the pan, and set aside. Add the salt pork, onion, green pepper, tomatoes, potatoes, catfish trimmings, Worcestershire sauce, Tabasco sauce, celery salt, salt, and water, and bring to a boil over high heat. Reduce the heat to low, cover tightly, and simmer for 30 minutes. Remove the catfish trimmings and discard. Add the catfish fillets and the reserved bacon and mix well. Cover the casserole tightly and continue to simmer over low heat until the fillets flake easily with a fork. Serve over hot rice.

4 servings

Determination

. . . "One day, while at work in the coal-mine, I happened to overhear two miners talking about a great school for colored people here in Virginia. . . . [It] seemed to me that it must be the greatest place on earth, not even heaven presented more attractions for me at that time than did the Hampton Normal and Industrial Institute in Virginia. . . . I resolved at once to go to that school, although I had no idea where it was, or how many miles away, or how I was going to reach it; I remember only that I was on fire constantly, and that was to go to Hampton. . . .

"Hampton, I learned . . . was an institution where [I] could study, could have a chance to work for [my] board, and at the same time be taught how to work and to realize the dignity of labor. . . . Perhaps the thing that touched and pleased me most in connection with my starting for Hampton was the interest that many of the older colored people took in the matter. . . . Some . . . [gave] a nickel, others a quarter, or a handkerchief. . . . They had spent the best days of their lives in slavery, and hardly expected to live to see the time when they would see a member of their own race leave home to attend a boarding school. . . . The distance from Malden to Hampton is about five hundred miles. I had not been away from home many hours before it began to grow painfully evident that I did not have enough money to pay my fare to Hampton. . . .

". . . One experience I shall long remember. I had been travelling over the mountains most of the afternoon in an old-fashioned stagecoach, when, late in the evening, the coach stopped for the night in a common, unpainted house called a hotel. . . . All the other passengers had been shown rooms and were getting ready for supper.

". . . [That] season in the mountains of Virginia was cold, and I wanted to get indoors for the night. . . . [The] man at the desk firmly refused to even consider the matter of providing me with food or lodging. This was my first experience in finding out what the color of my skin meant. My whole soul was . . . so bent on reaching Hampton that I did not have time to cherish any bitterness toward the hotel-keeper. By walking, begging rides both in wagons and in the cars . . . after a number of days, I reached Richmond, Virginia, about 82 miles from Hampton. . . .

"I was tired, I was hungry, I was anything but discouraged. I came upon a portion of the street where the board sidewalk was considerably elevated. I waited for a few minutes, till I was sure that no passers-by could see me, and then crept under the sidewalk and lay for the night upon the ground, with my satchel of clothing for a pillow. . . . I reached Hampton with a surplus of exactly fifty cents with which to begin my education. To me it had been a long and eventful journey too; but the first sight of the large, three-story, brick school building seemed to have rewarded me for all I had undergone in order to reach . . . Hampton. . . . It seemed to be the largest and most beautiful building I had ever seen. The sight of it seemed to give me new life. I felt that a new kind of existence had now begun. That life had new meaning. . . . If the people who gave the money to provide that building could appreciate the influence the sight of it had upon me, as well as thousands of other youths, they would feel all the more encouraged to make such gifts.

"As soon as possible after reaching the grounds of the Hampton Institute, I presented myself before the head teacher [Miss Mary F. Mackie] for assignment to a class. Having been so long without proper food, a bath, and a change of clothing, I did not, of course, make a very favourable impression upon her, and I could see at once that there were doubts in her mind about the wisdom of admitting me as a student. . . . In reaching Hampton, I felt I had reached the promised land, and I resolved to let no obstacle prevent me from putting forth the highest effort to fit myself to accomplish the most good in the world.

"For some time [Miss Mackie] did not refuse to admit me, neither did she decide in my favour, and I continued to linger about her, and to impress her in all the ways I could with my worthiness. In the meantime I saw her admitting other students, and that added greatly to my discomfort, for I felt, deep down in my heart, that I could only get a chance to show what was in me. . . . After some hours had passed . . . Miss Mackie said to me: 'the adjoining recitation-room needs sweeping. Take the broom and sweep it.' . . . I swept the recitation-room three times. Then I got a dusting-cloth and dusted it four times. All the woodwork around the walls, every bench, table, and desk. Besides, every piece of furniture had been moved and every closet and corner in the room had been thoroughly cleaned. . . .

"I had the feeling that in a large measure my future depended upon the impression I made upon the teacher in the cleaning of that room. When I was through, I reported to the head teacher. She was a 'Yankee' woman who knew just where to look for dirt. . . . [She] took out her handkerchief and rubbed it on the woodwork, about the walls, and over the table and benches. When she was unable to find one bit of dirt on the floor, one particle of dust on any of the furniture, she quietly remarked, " 'I guess you will do to enter Hampton.' "

—Booker T. Washington, Hampton, Class of 1875

SHE-CRAB SOUP

4	quarts water	2	cups heavy cream
2	tablespoons salt	⅛	teaspoon Worcestershire sauce
18	live blue she-crabs with roe (about ½ pound each)	⅛	teaspoon cayenne pepper
2½	tablespoons butter	⅛	teaspoon ground nutmeg
½	cup minced onion		Salt to taste
1	tablespoon flour	1	tablespoon pale dry sherry
2	cups milk		Chopped parsley, for garnish

In an 8- to 10-quart pot, bring 4 quarts of water and the salt to a boil. Add the crabs to the pot and allow the water to come to a second boil. Reduce the heat to low and simmer for 15 minutes. Drain the crabs and allow to cool; then remove the crabmeat and roe. Carefully remove as much shell and cartilage from the meat as possible.

In a 3- to 4-quart saucepan, melt the butter over medium heat. Sauté the onion in melted butter until tender. Add the flour, stirring constantly, and cook for an additional 3 minutes. Remove from the heat and gradually stir in the milk. Add the cream, crabmeat, and roe. Add the Worcestershire sauce and remaining spices. Simmer for 15 minutes, stirring occasionally. Just prior to serving, stir in the sherry. Garnish individual servings with chopped parsley.

4 servings

Raising the Walls

*"Dear schoolmates, the whole responsibility is upon us. . . . We are to raise, as it
were, her walls higher, year by year; therefore, let us work with unwearied zeal . . ."*

—Address of Welcome, composed and delivered at Hampton School Commencement,
by Alice P. Davis, June 12, 1873

"The story of the [choir's fundraising] campaign . . . must be told, and I have taken the
outline of it from . . . notes regularly kept by [them]. The [students] started upon it under
the care of General Armstrong, who has gone with them over most of their routes,
Mr. Fenner the musical director, and Mrs. S.T. Hooper, of Boston. . . ."

—Mary Frances Armstrong

". . . The idea of utilizing [Hampton student's] wonderful musical talents for [fundrais-
ing] had for years been a favorite one with the Principal, but the honor of first turning
to account this peculiar power is due to Professor George L. White, of Fisk University,
Tennessee, under the care of the American Missionary Association. . . . The world-
renowned 'Jubilee Singers' need no introduction.

"At Hampton no special effort had been made in this direction, chiefly because of
the great difficulty of finding a leader in all respects fitted for the peculiar demands of the
undertaking. But, as is often the case, the hour that brought the supreme necessity brought
also the man and the means to meet it.

"Mr. Thomas P. Fenner, of Providence, came to Hampton in June 1872, to estab-
lish a department of music. . . . He was quickly impressed . . . and entered into the labor
of organizing the 'Hampton Students' with an enthusiasm and skill that brought them
into the field ready for action within six months. . . . The Hampton Student Singers at
first numbered seventeen. As they were all young, and, with one exception, entirely unused
to appearing before the public, it was necessary to take out a large chorus until experience should develop the most available voices. . . . Five hundred dollars were given by one
who has often proved a friend in need to aid the company at the start. . . . At the right
time came the donation, and the Hampton Singers were launched. . . ."

—Helen W. Ludlow, Hampton teacher

"... We started from Hampton, on a cold and rainy evening, on the 13th of February, for Washington, D.C., where we gave our first concert, in Lincoln Hall, on the 15th. We were hospitably entertained in Washington at Howard University, by the kindness of General O. O. Howard. . . . [President Grant] made a few encouraging remarks to us, wishing us all possible success. General Armstrong told him something about our school, and introduced us to the President, who kindly shook hands with each of us. . . ."

—Hampton Student Singer, 1873

"... Little by little, [the] building grew; money and helping hands came from the north; a hundred acres of good farm-land gave opportunity for that practical education in agriculture so sadly needed throughout the South; and although the struggle was unceasing the spirit of those on whom the burden fell never for a moment flagged. . . ."

—Mary Frances Armstrong

And these students worked their way through school other students continued to "sing up" funds for additional industrial building.

"... February 17th. We visited the national Capitol, and saw those grand pictures and sights which I had never seen before. Up in the dome we sang 'The Church of God' and 'Wide River,' to see how it would sound. The effect was much greater than we had expected, and many people gathered below in the rotunda and applauded us. . . . One more concert, which was still more encouraging in numbers and enthusiasm, closed the first series in Washington and the company started hopefully upon their Northern tour. . . ."

—Hampton Student Singer, 1873

"... [The Hampton Singers] take their school-books with them to improve what chances for study they can secure, and are anxious to get back to Hampton to finish the course of education that has been interrupted, willingly and conscientiously, for the good of their people. . . ."

—Helen W. Ludlow, Hampton teacher

February 1873

Concerts and Work in Churches
During the Month

- 15*th*. Washington, D.C. Lincoln Hall.
- 18*th*. Washington, D.C. Lincoln Hall.
- 19*th*. Washington, D.C. Lincoln Hall.
- 23*rd*. Philadelphia. Dr. Hawes's Church (Presbyterian). Collection.
- 25*th*. Philadelphia. Horticultural Hall.
- 27*th*. Philadelphia. Dr. Warren's (M. E.) Church. Collection.
- 28*th*. Philadelphia. Horticultural Hall.

While the Hampton Student Singers toured the country, raising money, both buiding and "education for life" continued back home at Hampton.

A Hampton Student

". . . I have spoken of my own experience in entering the Hampton Institute. Perhaps few, if any, had anything like the same experience that I had . . . but about that same period there were hundreds who found their way to Hampton . . . after experiencing something of the same. . . ."

"The chance of the slave was very limited, you know, toward obtaining an education. I recollect I used to try and count a hundred. The way I did, I took a board and a piece of fire-coal, making marks one by one. At the surrender I could count fifty; that was my improvement from the time I commenced up to the surrender. . . . In the fall of 1866 the colored people started a school. I went to school that fall and was very proud to go. Such a scene I had never witnessed before; therefore, I made the best use of my time. The first week I learned the alphabet and commenced spelling and reading in the National Primer. I went to school some days and nights.

"I went to school till I got so I could read and write a little, then I had to stay home and wait on my sick father, but I went to night-school. I kept up studying my books, and then began to teach school, studying also nights. So you see this is the way I obtained what education I had before I came to Hampton. . . .

"Many nights I sat up till twelve o'clock over my lessons. In this way, I remained in school several months. . . . Then I heard of the Hampton Normal School, and determined to try to go to it. My father said he was not able to send me, so I could not go that term, but I did not lose my determination to get an education. . . . Knowing that my father was unable to send me [to Hampton], I saved all the money I could get, and got my friends to help me, so the next year I started for here.

"If I [am] successful in getting through here, I expect to spend the rest of my time in the elevation of my race. . . ."

—Hampton Student

"All last winter, which was an unusually severe one for Virginia, one of our students . . . in spite of lameness, walked sixteen miles, every day, in all weathers, over a rough road, for his schooling, and his sister bore him company. . . ."

—Mary Frances Armstrong

". . . We think a great deal of our Sunday night singing now, with our choir and our 600 voices, and our visitors from the Hygeia; but there was singing in those days, I can tell you. . . . When our little school of 86 students came together in that dark old room, with its one kerosene lamp near the platform, and sang with swaying bodies and beating feet, the music that came from their very souls, the hope and belief of the old slave life from which they had just come, mingling in it with the exultation of the freedom into which they had just entered. . . .

" 'Nobody knows de Trouble I'se seen' meant something real and tangible to every student in the school then; so did 'My Lord Delivered Daniel,' 'De Winter'll Soon be Over,' and all the other songs that our students today sing so glibly and with so little thought."

—Alice M. Bacon, Hampton student and teacher, 1894

CRAB BISQUE

2 tablespoons butter	¼ teaspoon thyme
1¼ cups finely chopped yellow onion	⅛ teaspoon ground nutmeg
1 cup finely chopped celery	3 cups clam juice
1 cup chopped red bell pepper	½ cup peeled and diced russet potatoes
1 small bay leaf	¾ cup light cream
1½ teaspoons Old Bay Seafood Seasoning (see page 110)	2 tablespoons Scotch whiskey
½ teaspoon cayenne pepper	1 pound lump crabmeat
	Salt and black pepper to taste
	Chopped chives, for garnish

Over medium heat, melt the butter in a heavy 2- to 3-quart pot. Add the onion, celery, red pepper, bay leaf, and next four seasoning ingredients. Cover and simmer for 10 minutes, stirring occasionally to prevent sticking. Add the clam juice and potatoes; bring to a boil. Reduce the heat, partially cover, and simmer until the potatoes are very tender. Purée the soup in a blender until smooth. Return the purée mixture to the pot and add the cream, Scotch, and crabmeat; season with salt and pepper. Garnish individual servings with chopped chives.

4 servings

CRAWFISH BISQUE

6 cups water	¼ cup flour
1 teaspoon salt, divided	⅛ teaspoon ground white pepper
48 live crawfish	⅛ teaspoon cayenne pepper
5 cups chicken broth	1 bay leaf
¼ cup (½ stick) butter	1 tablespoon sherry
¾ cup minced onion	Parsley, finely chopped, for garnish
1 leek, white part only, chopped fine	Red caviar, for garnish

Bring 6 cups of water and ½ teaspoon of the salt to a boil in a saucepan and immediately add the crawfish. Bring to a second boil, lower the heat, and simmer for 15 minutes; then drain, reserving the liquid. Separate the heads and tails from the crawfish. Remove the fat from the heads. Devein the tails and remove the meat. Refrigerate eighteen of the cleaned heads along with their meat and fat for future use. Return the reserved liquid, remaining heads, and chicken broth to the pot. Bring to a boil, reduce the heat, and simmer over medium heat. In a large pot with a tight-fitting lid, melt the butter over low heat; sauté the onion and leek, and blend in the flour, salt, and peppers. Heat until the mixture bubbles, then remove from the heat. With a slotted spoon, remove the heads from the simmering broth. Gradually add the broth to the flour mixture, stirring constantly until smooth. Add the bay leaf and crawfish meat; reduce the heat to low, cover, and simmer for 15 to 20 minutes. Return the boiled heads to the pot. Stir in sherry, and garnish individual servings with parsley and caviar.

6 to 8 servings

OYSTER STEW

*"... The one amusement is the water, I go out almost every day in the rowboat,
up under the bridge .... or along the coast to the mouth of the James River
and the oyster bar where the fat oysters grow."*

—from *Memories of Old Hampton,*
Miss Woolsey's letter of February 2, 1872

1½	quarts fresh-shucked oysters and their liquor	1½	teaspoons salt
2	cups milk	¼	teaspoon cayenne pepper
3	cups heavy cream	1	tablespoon sherry
⅓	cup butter		Parsley sprigs, for garnish
			Red caviar, for garnish

Pick over the oysters to remove any shell particles, then drain them, reserving their liquid. In a large saucepan, heat the reserved liquor. When the liquid is hot, but not boiling, add the milk and cream; stir well, and continue to heat without boiling. Just prior to serving, melt the butter in a large skillet over medium-high heat. When it begins to brown, add the drained oysters and sear over high heat for 3 to 5 minutes. Add the oysters to the milk mixture. Stir in the sherry. Garnish with parsley sprigs and float a small amount of caviar on top of the oyster stew.

4 servings

SOUTHERN SEAFOOD SOUP

Fresh okra fried in bacon drippings, and garden fresh vegetables infuse this soup with its "down home" southern flavor. Prepare enough for seconds!

3	cups fresh okra	½	teaspoon ground cumin
3	tablespoons bacon drippings	½	teaspoon seasoned salt
2	large onions, chopped fine	2	tablespoons solid shortening
1	large green bell pepper, seeded and coarsely chopped	¼	cup flour
		5	tomatoes, seeded and coarsely chopped
3	garlic cloves, chopped fine	1	pound lump crabmeat
½	cup diced ham	2	pounds cleaned large shrimp
2	quarts chicken stock	1	pint oysters with liquor
½	teaspoon ground allspice		

Season the okra to taste. In a large pot, over medium heat, fry the okra in the bacon drippings. Add the onions, green pepper, garlic, and ham. Fry until the onions are transparent. Add the chicken stock and next three ingredients. In a separate frying pan, melt the shortening over high heat. Add the flour and stir until a reddish brown roux forms—be careful not to burn it. Then quickly add the tomatoes with their liquid, stir, and add to the soup pot. Allow to simmer for 1 hour. Five minutes before serving, add the crabmeat, shrimp, and oysters. Mix well and ladle into individual serving bowls.

6 servings

Early Students' Reminiscences

"I saw General Armstrong the first day he put a foot in Hampton. . . . I was going to school down at the old Butler School when General Armstrong came. . . . The Butler School had four wings. All the wings opened on to a big meeting room in the center. I attended this school in 1865. Butler's camp was between Butler School and Soldier's Home. It was right here that Butler made up the Second and Tenth Calvary out of the Negroes entirely. . . . Armstrong wanted to start up independently. Butler had charge of everything except the farm which sits where the school sits now. The farm belonged to Senator Seagar; so the whole farm was transferred to General Armstrong. . . . Anyway, Armstrong began Hampton out of the best classes from Butler. . . . I worked at the Institute for thirty years and was pensioned from the Hampton Institute. . . ."

—Robert Ellett, former slave, b. 1849

"I came to Hampton as a student in October of 1871. . . . The only buildings here now (1909) that were there then are General Armstrong's house, Academic, Grigg's Hall, the reconstructed 'Uncle Tom's Cabin,' and Mr. Howe's house. . . .

"The Principal's house was the teacher's home as well as the General's. Academic Hall, standing where the present one stands, but one story less in height, held not only the class-rooms and assembly room but the Principal's Office, the Treasurer's Office, the Library, and afterwards the Printing Office. . . .

"Mr. Howe's house held two families, his own and that of General Marshall, our treasurer. Mr. Tolman, our Chaplain, lived in one wing of Bethesda Chapel, which was used as the school church and stood in the National Soldier's Cemetery. . . ."

—George J. Davis, Hampton, Class of 1874

SAFFRON MUSSEL SOUP

4 pounds well-scrubbed
   mussels
1¼ cups dry white wine
2 cups chicken broth
1 large leek, chopped fine
2 shallots, chopped fine
1 garlic clove, minced
1 celery rib, diced

¼ teaspoon curry powder
1 teaspoon saffron threads
2 tablespoons unsalted butter
2 cups heavy cream
1 cup crème fraîche (available at
   specialty food shops and some
   supermarkets)

Scrub the mussels well in several changes of cold water; scrape off the beards, and rinse the mussels again. In a large saucepan, combine the wine and mussels, and cook, covered, over medium-high heat, shaking the pan for 5 to 7 minutes, or until the mussells open. Discard any unopened mussels. Shell the mussels, reserving twelve half shells and twelve large mussels. Discard unused shells, and place the unreserved mussels in a fine sieve or colander lined with a double thickness of dampened paper towels. Strain the cooking liquid through into a bowl.

Set the mussels aside and return the cooking liquid to the saucepan. Add the chicken broth, leek, shallots, garlic, celery, spices, and butter. Simmer for 20 minutes. In a food processor, purée the mixture in batches, return it to the saucepan, and reduce it to 4½ cups. Add the heavy cream and crème fraîche and boil the mixture until it thickens. Add the mussels and warm the soup over moderately low heat, stirring, until mussels are heated through. Ladle the soup into six bowls, garnishing each with two mussels on the half shell and several saffron threads.

6 to 8 servings

". . . In undertaking any great work . . . it is a wise as well as a fair policy to let a brave beginning appeal to [public] sympathies at once, as the pledge of an honest purpose, and its honest fulfillment. It is on this principle that the building of Virginia Hall has been carried out. Its foundations were laid early in April of last year. At that time there was not a dollar in the treasury for building purposes, and $3000 were owing for bricks which had been manufactured the previous summer.

"The chorus of Hampton Students had just started upon their untried campaign for the $75,000 estimated as the full cost, and the future certainly seemed difficult to read. 'Break ground' was the decision, 'and let the work go on as long as the money comes in. It is a great need, and the Lord knows it. We will do all in our power, and then if He can afford to wait, we can.'

"The ground was broken, accordingly, as soon as the frost was sufficiently out of it, and the work pushed, until, on June 12th, 1873, the corner-stone was laid by Prof. Roswell D. Hitchcock, D.D., of New-York, in the presence of many distinguished visitors from the North and South, and Great Britain, who were drawn to Hampton by the interest of the occasion, and of the commencement exercises of the school, and by their desire to inspect the successful operation of the manual-labor system in Southern education.

"In announcing the design of the new hall, Gen. Armstrong said: 'As security for its completion, we have our faith in our own earnest efforts, in the people of this country, and in our God.' . . .

"As fast as the dollars have come into the treasury, they have been turned into bricks and mortar and timber, and the work has not been suspended for want of them for even a single day. As a friend lately remarked: 'There is something actually sublime in the way those walls have gone steadily up, rising day after day, day after day, right through this panic, when the largest business firms have been brought to a stand-still. It is like the movement of God's providence.' . . .

"The material of the building is red brick, the color relieved by lines and cappings of black. . . . It will contain a chapel, with seating capacity for four hundred people; an industrial-room for the manufacture of clothing, and for instruction in sewing in all its branches; a dining-room able to accommodate two hundred and seventy-five boarders; a large laundry and kitchen, besides quarters for twelve teachers, and sleeping-rooms for one hundred and twenty girls.

"The heating apparatus is to be steam, which will be applied to cooking. The kitchen and laundry are to have the best appliances for thorough work, and are to be as attractive and comfortable as any rooms on the premises. Every thing will be done to dignify labor, by making its associations respectable.

"Gas will be introduced as soon as possible. The basement . . . will be well lighted, dry, and besides containing the printing-office and being the publication office of the *Southern Workman,* will be useful in many ways.

"For months past, every nerve of the corps of Hampton's workers has been strained to secure funds for the completion of their beautiful building.

"The first $40,000 have been given and nearly expended, ten thousand of which have been the direct net proceeds of the concerts of the 'Hampton Students' and the remaining thirty thousand the indirect results of the interest they have excited, or the fruits of the collateral efforts that have been made. The workers are now upon the home-stretch. With no discouraging debt[.] . . . Twenty-five thousand dollars more must be secured to prepare it for use next fall, and many young women eager for education are watching with anxious eyes for its opening. It is for this that our Hampton Student Singers have once more entered the field, and that we send this little book out with them."

—Samuel Armstrong

Hampton singers
(Courtesy of Hampton University Archives)

Concerts and Work in Churches
During the Month

- 1*st.* Philadelphia. Horticultural Hall. Matinée.
- 3*rd.* Philadelphia. Central Congregational Church. Concert.
- 4*th.* Philadelphia. Dr. Furness's Church. Concert.
- 5*th.* Philadelphia. Athletic Hall.
- 6*th.* Germantown. Association Hall.
- 7*th.* New-York. Steinway Hall.
- 9*th.* New-York. Dr. Burchard's (Presbyterian) Church. Collection taken.
- 10*th.* New-York. Fourth-ave. Presbyterian Church (Dr. Crosby's).
- 11*th.* New-York. Steinway Hall.
- 14*th.* New-York. Steinway Hall.
- 15*th.* New-York. Union League Hall. Matinée.
- 16*th.* New-York. West Twenty-third Street Presbyterian Church. Collection.
- 18*th.* Bridgeport (CT). Opera House.
- 20*th.* New-York. Dr. Rogers's (Reformed) Church. Concert.
- 21*st.* New-York. All Souls Church (Dr. Bellows's). Concert.
- 22*nd.* New York. Union League Hall. Matinée.
- 23*rd.* New-York. Dr. Anderson's (Baptist) Church.
- 23*rd.* New-York. Memorial Church (Dr. C. S. Robinson's). Collection.
- 24*th.* New-York. Steinway Hall.
- 27*th.* New-York. Steinway Hall.
- 29*th.* New-York. Union League Hall. Matinée.
- 30*th.* New-York. Church of the Messiah (Dr. Powell's, Unitarian). Collection.
- 31*st.* Brooklyn, Lafayette Avenue Presbyterian Church (Dr. Cuyler's). Concert.

VEGETABLE BEEF SOUP

When coastal waters turn winter gray, this hearty vegetable soup will warm you with reminders of spring planting, fragrant summer gardens, and autumn's bountiful harvest.

2 pounds beef stew meat, cubed	1 large turnip, peeled and diced into
Seasoned salt and black	¼-inch sections
pepper to taste	4 carrots, sliced diagonally
3 tablespoons vegetable oil	½ pound green beans, cut into 1½-inch
1 medium onion, diced	pieces
1 celery stalk, sliced into ⅛- to	4 medium new potatoes, quartered
¼-inch pieces	¼ teaspoon dried thyme
5 cups beef broth	¾ cup frozen corn
5 cups chicken broth	⅔ cup minced fresh parsley leaves
3 cups water	
1 14- to 16-ounce can tomatoes,	
undrained and chopped	

Season the beef with seasoned salt and pepper to taste and set aside. In a large, heavy kettle, heat the oil over high heat until smoke just begins to rise, add the beef, and reduce the heat to medium high. Add the onion and celery. Cook until the meat is brown on all sides. Add the beef broth, chicken broth, and water. Bring the liquid to a boil and simmer, uncovered, for 1½ hours, or until the meat is tender; occasionally skim away the froth and add additional water to prevent sticking. Next, add the tomatoes and their liquid. Add the next four ingredients and cook for another 20 to 30 minutes, or until the vegetables are tender. Stir in the thyme and add additional seasoned salt and pepper to taste. Stir in the corn and parsley and simmer for an additional minute.

4 to 6 servings

SWEET POTATO SOUP

2	lean bacon slices	3	large sweet potatoes, peeled and sliced thin
1	medium onion, sliced thin	2	large russet potatoes, peeled and sliced thin
1	cup finely chopped celery	2	cups light cream
1	tablespoon minced garlic	1	cup whipping cream, for garnish
¼	teaspoon ground cumin	¼	cup thinly sliced green onions, for garnish
1	bay leaf		
3	cups chicken stock		
⅓	cup dry white wine		

In a medium saucepan over medium heat, fry the bacon until it is crisp, then transfer it to a paper towel-lined plate to drain. Sauté the onion, celery, and garlic in the drippings. Add the cumin and bay leaf. Stir and allow to cook for an additional 5 minutes. Add the stock, wine, and potatoes, and bring to a boil. Reduce the heat to medium low, cover, and simmer for an additional 25 to 30 minutes or until the potatoes are tender. Discard the bay leaf. In a blender, purée the potatoes (may require two separate batches), add light cream, and simmer over low heat. Season to taste. The soup may be thinned with the addition of chicken broth, if desired. Prior to serving, whip the cream until it holds a soft peak. Ladle the soup into bowls and garnish with a dollop of whipped cream and green onions.

4 to 6 servings

Hampton Teachers Reminisce

Those who came to educate were as committed to the process and the school as the students who sacrificed all to attend were. In 1868, shortly after General Grant's election to the presidency, Jane Stuart Woolsey went to Hampton to open an industrial room. Others followed her, some giving up prestigious teaching positions at schools such as Vassar.

"The life of a teacher in those early days was very plain . . . but interest in the work of teaching those . . . just out of slavery was so absorbing that I remember being sorry when the long summer vacation came . . . an experience never repeated in my life as a teacher. . . .

". . . [At] least one of the men in the first [Hampton] class was thirty years old, and not a few were over twenty, so that they brought with them a personal consciousness of what it was to be a slave. . . ."

—Susan B. Harrold, Hampton teacher, 1894

"I never saw more earnest seekers after knowledge. I did my office work in the schoolroom, and as long as I remained, generally until it was dark, they stayed also, digging over the books or working their mathematics on the blackboard. . . ."

—Mary F. Mackie, Hampton teacher, 1894

". . . The "teacher's home" numbered eight ladies. . . . They were Miss Bacon, Miss Woolsey, Miss Charlotte Mackie, Miss Gertrude Hyde, Miss Tyler, Miss Parrish, Miss Harrold, and Miss Bacon's little sister, the Junior Professor as she was playfully nicknamed. . . . The Academic Department was put in shape by Rebecca Bacon . . . [a] noble worker among the pioneers to whom Hampton owes much."

—Mary F. Mackie, Hampton teacher, 1894

". . . December 1869—General Armstrong is very busy . . . and goes north to raise money for the school, Miss Bacon [Rebecca T.] has entire charge [and] is thoroughly capable. . . . The whole routine of the school, the course of instruction, the division into classes, the assigning of teachers to classes . . . and the weekly instruction have been her work so far, and it is well done. . . ."

—Miss Jane Stuart Woolsey, Hampton teacher, 1894

"In the early days of the Hampton School the great question agitating the Teacher's Home was not beefsteak or lamb chops, nor yet early dinner or late, but was simply how, by hook or crook, to secure enough food and ensure its being prepared as well as the poor material at hand would permit."

—Alice M. Bacon, Hampton student and teacher, 1894

"Miss Caroline Thomas manages the housekeeping department very skillfully. She is full of sweetness as well as good sense and makes a gracious ladies' atmosphere in the place. . . . Everything is good and abundant and to give an instance take today's bill of fare in the teacher's home."

—Sunday, December 12, 1869

Breakfast—Salt mackerel,
minced beef, white potatoes,
sweet potatoes, cornbread,
wheat bread, coffee, excellent
black tea, and chocolate; griddle
cakes (with syrup) plenty of
them hot; butter, milk
and cream

Dinner—Cold roast turkey,
cold goose, mashed potatoes,
cranberry sauce, dressed
salad, corn and wheat
bread, lemon custard,
vanilla blancmange, cream

Tea—Stewed oysters,
milk toast, stewed apples
and cherries, bread butter,
tea, chocolate, cream

Miss Thomas always gives us a pitcher of cream, thick and sweet. This fare is in contrast with dumplings and grease for dinner, and grease and dumplings for tea, at seven dollars a week, which have been my portion on some occasions.

OKRA SOUP

¼ pound slab bacon, diced	2 pounds fresh okra
1 large onion, chopped coarse	4 large tomatoes, peeled, seeded, and chopped coarse
2 garlic cloves, minced	1 large bay leaf
2 quarts chicken stock	⅛ teaspoon ground cumin
2–3 pounds meaty beef shank bones	Pinch of powdered saffron
¼ cup diced ham	

In a large saucepan, heat the bacon until transparent; add the onion and garlic and sauté until the onion is transparent. Add the chicken stock and shank bones, and bring to a boil over high heat. Reduce the heat to medium low, cover, and simmer for 2 hours. Extract the soup bones from the pot and cut the meat away from the bones, discarding the bones; dice the meat and return it to the pot. Stir in the ham, okra, tomatoes, bay leaf, cumin, and saffron. Bring to a boil over high heat. Reduce the heat to moderate, cover, and simmer for 2 hours. Discard the bay leaf prior to serving.

6 servings

VIRGINIA CREAM OF PEANUT SOUP

¼ cup (½ stick) butter	¼ teaspoon salt
1 medium onion, chopped fine	⅛ teaspoon cayenne pepper
¼ cup chopped celery	1 cup light cream
2 teaspoons flour	¼ cup skinless, unsalted peanuts, coarsely ground, for garnish
2 quarts chicken broth	
1 cup smooth peanut butter	

In a 3- to 4-quart saucepan, melt the butter over low heat. Add the onion and celery, and sauté until transparent. Add the flour and blend until the mixture is lump-free. Slowly add the chicken broth, continue to stir, and bring to a boil. Blend in the peanut butter; add the spices, and simmer for approximately 15 minutes. Just prior to serving, stir in the cream and garnish individual servings with ground peanuts.

6 to 8 servings

CREAM OF TOMATO SOUP

1 pound fresh tomatoes, peeled, seeded, and chopped	3 tablespoons unsalted butter
	Salt and white pepper to taste
½ cup water	2 teaspoons baking soda
2 cups half-and-half	1 teaspoon brown sugar
2 cups milk	Fresh basil, for garnish

In a medium saucepan, stew the tomatoes in the water for 30 minutes. In the top of a double boiler, heat the half-and-half, milk, and butter until the butter melts. Add salt and pepper. Just prior to serving, add the soda and sugar to the tomatoes. Pour the tomatoes into the cream-butter mixture. Ladle into individual serving dishes and garnish with basil.

4 to 6 servings

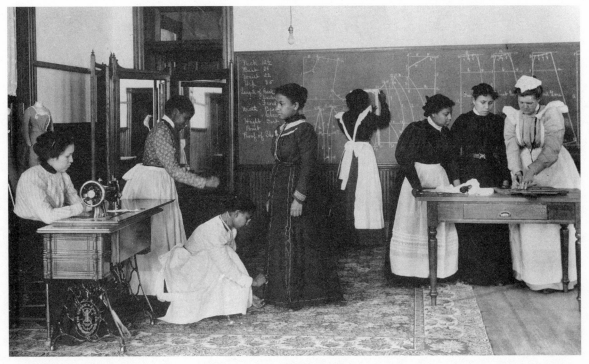

A class in dress making
"In addition to the special work of this department, the girls are taught the ordinary duties of a household, laundry-work etc. . . . " —Mary Frances Armstrong, Hampton Teacher, 1894 *(Reproduced from the collections of the Library of Congress)*

While the Hampton Student Singers toured the country, raising money, both building and "education for life" continued back home at Hampton. "The young women of the school were provided with an Industrial Department following the generous donation of a northern patron. Here they were taught to cut and fit garments, and use various sewing machines," said Mary Frances Armstrong. The garments they made were sold to members of the school and members of the community. "One of the fundamental principles of the school was that nothing should be given which can be earned or in any way supplied by the pupil, and in insonance with this principle, regular personal expenses for board, etc., rated at $10 a month, are thrown upon each student, to be paid by them, half in cash and half in labor."

SHERRIED CREAM OF MUSHROOM SOUP

2½	pounds fresh mushrooms with stems*	½	teaspoon salt
½	cup (1 stick) butter, divided	2	cups chicken broth
¼	cup finely chopped shallots	2	cups half-and-half
3	tablespoons flour	1½	cups dry sherry
⅛	teaspoon dry mustard	2	cups heavy cream, whipped, for garnish
¼	teaspoon onion powder		Chopped chives, for garnish
	Pinch of nutmeg (⅟₁₆ teaspoon)		

Clean and chop 2 pounds of the mushrooms with stems. In a medium saucepan, melt ¼ cup of the butter. Sauté the mushrooms and shallots. Blend in the flour, spices, and chicken broth. Stir until smooth, then transfer to the top of a double boiler, add the half-and-half, and cook very slowly over low heat for approximately 30 to 35 minutes. Clean, trim, and slice the remaining mushrooms and sauté in the remaining ¼ cup of butter. When the mushrooms are lightly browned, add the sherry. Remove from the heat and allow to stand for 5 minutes. Add to the mixture in the double boiler and mix well. Ladle into individual serving bowls. Garnish with a dollop of whipped cream and chopped chives.

   *Mushrooms should never be washed. Simply wipe them clean with a damp cloth.

4 to 6 servings

CUCUMBER SALAD

There is nothing quite as cool and refreshing on a hot summer day as the cool taste of cucumbers, fresh from the garden! This lightly dressed salad is a family favorite.

4	cups peeled and thinly sliced cucumbers	½	teaspoon sugar
1	onion, sliced thin	1	teaspoon dried dill weed
½	teaspoon salt	½	cup thinly sliced radishes
⅓	cup sour cream	1	tablespoon chopped fresh chives, for garnish
2	tablespoons vinegar		

Place the sliced cucumbers, onion, and salt in a paper-towel-lined colander and set aside to absorb excess moisture. Combine the sour cream, vinegar, sugar, and dill weed in a bowl, stirring until smooth. Add the cucumber mixture and radishes; toss gently. Cover and chill for 1 hour. Garnish with chopped chives just prior to serving.

6 to 8 servings

My First Sight of Hampton

". . . My first sight of Hampton was in the spring of 1871 at Easter. It was a case of love at first sight and familiarity has not bred contempt. . . ."

—Miss Mary F. Mackie, Hampton teacher, 1894

". . . One of the clearest pictures of that ten days visit was . . . of a golden-haired girl of twelve [Alice M. Bacon], pretty young I thought for a teacher. As a twig is bent the tree inclines proved true in her case. What her later work has been . . . I leave you to tell the sequel.

—Miss Mary F. Mackie, Hampton teacher, 1894

". . . In the years 1870 and 1871 [Hampton] was still an infant. Everything was new and unformed. There were few customs and precedent by which to go. . . . Of the students in the school at that time I cannot speak without real affection. Members of the Junior class were my pupils, the Seniors were my classmates, and with the Middlers I was on terms of friendly intimacy. . . ."

—Miss Alice M. Bacon, Hampton teacher and student, 1894

Due to the crowded classes and a small force of workers, Alice M. Bacon began her career as a school marm at the unprecedented early age of twelve. The "Little Professor" as she was fondly called, spent one year at the Hampton Institute with her sister, Rebecca T. Bacon, Assistant Principal of Hampton. When Rebecca left Hampton, Alice continued her studies at home. In 1881, she passed, in three subjects, the Harvard examination for women—a test of college-grade achievement.

In later years Alice M. Bacon would return to Hampton and continue to make tremendous contributions.

Tomatoes and Dressing

When purchasing tomatoes, look for firm fruit with no soft spots or mold. They should be stored at room temperature in the supermarket. Ripening stops once tomatoes have been chilled. If you have winter tomatoes at home that are not quite ripe, store them in a fruit dish or allow them to ripen at room temperature, stem end up and away from direct sunlight. If you keep them with an apple or pear—both of which give off a natural ripener called ethylene gas—they will ripen even faster.

4	large tomatoes	1	teaspoon salt
⅔	cup cider vinegar	1½	tablespoons sugar

Slice the tomatoes into a bowl. Mix the remaining ingredients, drizzle over the tomatoes, and chill well before serving.

6 to 8 servings

Warm Dandelion Salad and Baked Goat Cheese

Marinate the cheese the day before you want to serve this tangy salad.

½	cup olive oil	1	cup toasted fresh white bread crumbs
1	teaspoon dried thyme		Salt and black pepper to taste
½	teaspoon dried basil		
	24-ounce log soft, mild goat cheese, cut into four ½-inch-thick rounds		

In a small bowl, combine the first three ingredients and set aside. Arrange the cheese rounds on the bottom of a glass dish in a single layer. Pour the oil mixture over the cheese and turn gently to coat. Cover, refrigerate, and marinate overnight.

Preheat the oven to 450 degrees F. Remove the cheese from oil and coat with bread crumbs, pressing the crumbs gently into the cheese. Arrange the coated cheese rounds on a lightly oiled baking sheet. Bake until lightly bubbly and golden, approximately 5 minutes. Salt and pepper to taste and set aside.

RASPBERRY DRESSING

¼ cup fresh lemon juice
¼ cup raspberry vinegar
Salt and black pepper to taste

½ cup walnut oil
¼ cup olive oil

In a small bowl, whisk together the lemon juice and vinegar. Add salt and pepper to taste. Next, add the oils in a slow stream and whip until well blended but not emulsified. Microwave for 1 to 2 minutes just prior to dressing the salad.

WARM DANDELION SALAD

1 cup young, tender dandelion greens, washed, spun dry, and cut into bite-size pieces
2 cups bibb lettuce, washed, spun dry, and torn

¼ cup matchstick-cut carrots
2 tablespoons minced fresh chives
⅛ teaspoon minced garlic
¼ cup chopped walnuts
⅓ cup crumbled firm goat cheese

In a large bowl, toss together the salad greens, carrots, garlic, and chopped walnuts; top with warm goat cheese and drizzle with raspberry dressing.

4 generous servings

Mixed Garden Salad and Dressing

1	head bibb lettuce	2	cups cherry tomatoes, halved
1	head Belgian endive	2	shallots, sliced thin
1	small head iceberg lettuce	2	tablespoons chopped chives
2	cups tender spinach leaves	2	hard-boiled eggs, chopped coarse

Combine all ingredients, except the chopped eggs, in a large salad bowl and refrigerate. Just before serving, toss with Garden-Fresh Dressing (recipe below) and scatter the chopped eggs on top.

8 servings

GARDEN-FRESH DRESSING

2	large garlic cloves, crushed	1	teaspoon seasoned salt
⅔	cup virgin olive oil	¼	teaspoon paprika
⅔	cup tarragon vinegar	⅛	teaspoon cayenne pepper
¼	teaspoon garlic powder	¼	teaspoon freshly ground black
¼	teaspoon onion powder		pepper

In a cruet or suitably sized glass jar with a tight-fitting top, combine the above ingredients. Shake well and pour over the salad immediately before serving.

Yields 1⅓ cups

GARDEN HERB SALAD

1 medium cucumber
1 large head leaf lettuce
2 cups lightly packed spinach
   leaves
¼ cup lightly packed chopped
   fresh chives

1 tablespoon chopped fresh rosemary
3 tablespoons lightly packed chopped
   fresh basil
⅔ cup toasted walnut pieces
⅓ cup pine nuts
   Freshly ground black pepper

Peel the cucumber lengthwise in five strips, leaving strips of peel in between. Cut into thin slices. Place in a medium bowl. Tear the lettuce and spinach into the bowl; add the herbs. Cover and refrigerate until serving time. Just prior to serving, dress (see the recipe below) and garnish with walnuts, pine nuts and a twist of freshly ground pepper.

4 servings

DRESSING

¼ cup walnut oil
2 tablespoons vegetable oil
2 tablespoons cider vinegar

1 teaspoon water
⅛ teaspoon onion powder
   Pinch of seasoned salt

Combine all of the above ingredients in a small bowl and mix well. Dress the salad just prior to serving.

Yields ½ cup

SUMMER SALAD

2	vine ripened tomatoes, peeled, and cubed	½	cup seedless black olive halves
1	small cucumber, peeled and quartered	¼	cup sliced green onions
¼	cup Bermuda onion, chopped coarse	2	cups roasted chicken, cubed
		½	cup smoked ham, cubed
			Shredded lettuce

Combine all of the above ingredients, except lettuce. Place on a bed of coarsely shredded lettuce and top with dressing (see the recipe below).

4 servings

SUMMER SALAD DRESSING

½	cup vegetable oil	2	teaspoons grated onion
¼	cup homemade mayonnaise (see recipe on page 68; may substitute commercial)	⅓	cup vegetable juice
		1	teaspoon paprika
		½	teaspoon seasoned salt
¼	cup lemon juice	2	garlic cloves, minced
2½	tablespoons sugar	½	teaspoon minced chives

Combine the above ingredients in a glass cruet, cover tightly, and shake well.

Yields 1⅓ cups

OYSTER SALAD WITH VINAIGRETTE SAUCE

1   pint shucked oysters
2   cups sliced green onions
1   teaspoon Worcestershire
     sauce

2   hard-boiled eggs, chopped
     Shredded lettuce

Drain the liquid from the oysters into a medium saucepan. Over medium-high heat, poach the oysters in their own liquid until they are cooked through and their edges curl, approximately 3 minutes. Drain the oysters and combine with the remaining ingredients. Place on a bed of shredded lettuce and refrigerate. Top with Vinaigrette Sauce (see the recipe below) just prior to serving.

4 servings

VINAIGRETTE SAUCE

½   teaspoon Dijon mustard
½   teaspoon seasoned salt
¼   teaspoon white pepper
¼   cup red wine vinegar
¼   cup vegetable oil
½   cup olive oil

¼   teaspoon paprika
⅛   teaspoon cayenne pepper
1   garlic clove, minced
1   teaspoon lemon zest
1   tablespoon sour cream

In a medium bowl, combine the mustard, salt, and pepper. Add the vinegar and stir with a wire whisk until well mixed. Slowly, a drop at a time, whisk in the vegetable oil. Repeat the process with the olive oil. Add the remaining ingredients and pour over a well-chilled salad.

Yields 1 cup

ZESTY SHRIMP SALAD

3   pounds medium shrimp, boiled and shelled
½   cup sliced green onions, with tops
1½ cups halved cherry tomatoes
2   garlic cloves, minced
2   tablespoons lemon juice
¼   cup olive oil

¾   teaspoon dry mustard
¼   teaspoon onion powder
⅛   teaspoon cayenne pepper
    Lettuce leaves
    Salt and black pepper to taste
½   cup crumbled Feta cheese, for garnish

Place the boiled shrimp in a large bowl add the onions, tomatoes, and garlic. Toss together and refrigerate to chill. In a cruet or glass jar, combine the lemon juice, olive oil, mustard, onion powder, and cayenne pepper. Shake well and dress the salad. Arrange the salad on a bed of lettuce leaves. Salt and pepper to taste and garnish with Feta.

6 servings

SHRIMP SALAD

2   pounds shrimp, shelled and cleaned
1½ tablespoons Old Bay Seafood Seasoning (see page 110)
6   hard-boiled eggs, chopped coarse
⅓   cup finely chopped celery
1   medium onion, chopped fine
¼   cup sweet relish

2   tablespoons dill relish
2   tablespoons soft cream cheese
2   tablespoons mayonnaise
1   tablespoon sour cream
½   teaspoon dry mustard
½   teaspoon seasoned salt
¼   teaspoon paprika
⅛   teaspoon cayenne pepper

Clean the shrimp and set aside. In a large pot, bring 3 quarts of water to a boil over high heat. Add the Old Bay Seafood Seasoning and shrimp. Bring to a second boil. When done, shrimp should be pink and opaque, with their tails slightly curled. Remove them from the heat, drain immediately, and set aside. In a separate bowl, combine the remaining ingredients, mixing well. Add to the shrimp, mix well, and chill before serving.

4 servings

SEAFOOD SALAD

1 pound lump crabmeat	1 garlic clove, minced
1 pound medium shrimp, boiled, peeled, and deveined	¼ teaspoon seasoned salt
	⅛ teaspoon cayenne pepper
	⅛ teaspoon Tabasco sauce
3 hard-boiled eggs, chopped coarse	¼ cup sour cream
	¼ cup mayonnaise
¼ cup minced onion	Juice of ½ lemon
½ cup minced celery	¼ teaspoon lemon zest
3 tablespoons chopped green bell pepper	1 tablespoon capers, for garnish

Pick over the crabmeat, removing any foreign objects and cartilage. Place the crab and shrimp in a medium bowl. In a separate bowl, combine the remaining ingredients. Mix well. Pour over the salad, mix gently, and chill. Just prior to serving, sprinkle with capers.

4 to 6 servings

SHAD ROE SALAD

2   pounds shad roe
1   tablespoon vinegar
½   teaspoon salt
¼   cup minced celery

1   tablespoon chopped parsley
1   tablespoon chopped chives
½   cup peeled, diced cucumber

Cover the shad roe with water. Add the vinegar and salt and cook over low heat for about 10 minutes or until the roe is firm. Drain; remove membrane from the roe; gently separate the roe eggs with a fork and set aside. Add remaining ingredients to roe and mix with 2 tablespoons of the mayonnaise dressing (see recipe below). Serve immediately.

4 servings

MAYONNAISE DRESSING

2   egg yolks
½   cup olive oil
¼   teaspoon dry mustard
2   tablespoons lemon juice

½   teaspoon powdered sugar
    Pinch of cayenne pepper
½   teaspoon salt

In a small bowl, beat the egg yolks with a wire whisk or an electric mixer on high speed until lemon colored. While you beat the eggs, add the oil, drop by drop. Beat in the dry mustard, lemon juice, sugar, cayenne, and salt. Refrigerate. (Please note recent cautionary warnings with regard to the use of raw egg products. Feel free to substitute commercially prepared mayonnaise.)

Yields ¾ cup

FRESH SUMMER CRAB SALAD

1	pound lump crabmeat	⅛	teaspoon curry powder
½	cup minced celery	1	tablespoon Worcestershire sauce
½	cup finely chopped green onions	⅓	cup mayonnaise
1	garlic clove, minced	⅓	cup sour cream
½	teaspoon dry mustard	2	tablespoons fresh lemon juice
½	teaspoon lemon pepper		Lettuce leaves
1¼	teaspoons Old Bay Seafood Seasoning (see page 110)	4	hard-boiled eggs, quartered
		2	tomatoes, quartered
		2	lemons, quartered

Pick over the crabmeat, removing cartilage and any foreign material. In a medium bowl, mix the crabmeat and next eight ingredients. In a small bowl, combine the mayonnaise, sour cream, and lemon juice. Mix well and combine with the crab. Gently stir until just blended. Refrigerate to chill. Serve on a bed of lettuce leaves; garnish with egg and tomato quarters. Serve with lemon quarters.

4 servings

POTATO AND HAM SALAD

2	large baking potatoes	½	teaspoon fresh basil
½	cup cubed smoked ham	½	teaspoon fresh thyme
¾	cup sliced green onions	1	cup beef broth
¼	cup chopped Bermuda onion	1	tablespoon sugar
1	tablespoon chopped parsley	¼	cup cider vinegar
¼	teaspoon black pepper	1½	tablespoons all-purpose flour
¼	teaspoon celery seeds		

Boil the potatoes until just soft, remove from the water, and cool. Slice the potatoes approximately ¼ inch thick into a large bowl. Add the ham, onions, parsley, and remaining herbs and spices to the bowl. Gently mix these ingredients together. Combine the beef broth and sugar in a saucepan. Bring to a boil, reduce the heat, and simmer for 5 minutes. In a small bowl, whisk together the vinegar and flour until smooth; add to the beef broth mixture. Continue to simmer and stir for an additional 2 minutes and then pour over the potatoes, tossing lightly. Serve at room temperature.

4 to 6 servings

Coleslaw

5	cups grated cabbage	¼	cup mayonnaise
1½	cups grated carrot	1½	teaspoons sugar
2	teaspoons celery seeds	½	teaspoon onion powder
¾	cup dairy sour cream	½	teaspoon seasoned salt
2	tablespoons light cream		

In a large serving bowl, combine the first three ingredients. In a separate mixing bowl, combine the remaining dressing ingredients. Add to the cabbage mixture. Coat thoroughly with dressing and refrigerate overnight or at least 2 or 3 hours prior to serving.

8 to 10 servings

WHITE BEAN SALAD

2	16-ounce cans white beans, undrained	½	teaspoon ground cumin
½	cup water	⅛	teaspoon cayenne pepper
1	small onion, chopped	2	tablespoons olive oil
3	minced garlic cloves, divided		Salt and black pepper to taste
1	bay leaf	¼	cup chopped fresh parsley
½	cup fresh lemon juice	2	tomatoes, seeded, peeled, and diced

In a small to medium pot, combine the beans, water, onion, 1 garlic clove, and bay leaf. Stir well and bring to a quick boil. Simmer over low heat for 15 minutes. Drain the beans and reserve the liquid. Combine the lemon juice, remaining garlic cloves, seasonings, olive oil, ⅓ cup of reserved liquid, and salt and pepper to taste. Pour the mixture over the beans, mix gently, and refrigerate for several hours prior to serving. Just before serving, toss with the minced parsley and tomatoes.

4 to 6 servings

SPICY BLACK-EYED PEA AND TOMATO SALAD

Black-eyed peas are no longer relegated to duty as a traditional side dish served over rice and accompanied by "a mess of greens" and a hearty slice of cornbread. This spicy and delicious black-eyed-pea salad recipe casts this "Southern belle" of the pea family in a new and delicious light.

1	16-ounce can black-eyed peas, undrained	2	jalapeño peppers, seeded and minced fine
1	cup water	2	ripe tomatoes, coarsely diced
½	cup chopped onion		Salt and black pepper to taste
2	large garlic cloves, minced	¼	cup minced cilantro or parsley, for garnish
1	bay leaf		

Combine the black-eyed peas, water, onion, garlic, and bay leaf, and bring to a boil. Reduce the heat to low and simmer for 15 minutes. Drain the beans and discard the bay leaf. Toss together the salad and dressing (see recipes below); refrigerate for several hours prior to serving. Just before serving, add the minced cilantro or parsley, toss, and serve.

4 to 6 servings

DRESSING

⅓ cup fresh lemon juice
2   small garlic cloves, minced fine

½   teaspoon ground cumin
⅛   teaspoon cayenne pepper
½   cup olive oil

Combine the ingredients and use to dress salad.

Student plowing
On the farm, they grew what they needed and sold the excess. "Between twenty and thiry gallons of milk are supplied to the boarding department of the school or sold in the neighborhood, at an average price of thiry cents per gallon. In addition to their training on the farm and in the printing office, male students found employment in the blacksmith-shop and paint-shop among others." —Mary Frances Armstrong *(Reproduced from the collections of the Library of Congress)*

Booker T. Washington as a young man

"... I had the feeling that in a large measure my future depended upon the impression I made upon the teacher in the cleaning of that room. When I was through, I reported to the head teacher. She was a 'Yankee' woman who knew just where to look for dirt. She took out her handkerchief and rubbed it on the woodwork, about the walls, and over the table and benches. When she was unable to find one bit of dirt on the floor, one particle of dust on any of the furniture, she quietly remarked, 'I guess you will do to enter Hampton.' ... [N]ever did any youth pass an examination for entrance into Harvard or Yale that gave him more genuine satisfaction. I have passed several examinations since then, but I have always felt that this was the best one that I ever passed." —Booker T. Washington, Hampton, Class of 1875 *(Courtesy of Hampton University Archives)*

Striving for Excellence

"From the first Hampton has been true to the idea of education by self-help, and I hope that it will remain so. . . . The students get nothing but an opportunity to work."

"The thing to be done was clear: to train selected . . . youth who should go out and teach and lead their people first by example, by getting land and homes . . . to replace stupid drudgery with skilled hands, and to these ends, to build up an industrial system, for the sake of self-support and industrial labor, but also for the sake of character. . . . And inside every building students were striving for excellence as the Hampton system was employed with excellent results. At first there was no enthusiasm for the manual labor plan. People said it has been tried . . . elsewhere and given up. . . ."

—General Samuel C. Armstrong

As Hampton students graduated they began fulfilling General Armstrong's vision for the school. Returning to small towns all over the South they began teaching and making a difference in their community. In this way they often recruited other students—some of them still carrying the badge of slavery and yearning to learn.

Georgia Washington's Story

. . . Georgia Washington was taught and recruited for Hampton by recent Hampton graduate, Mr. Joseph Towe. Both her mother and father were slaves and, "My mother, brother and myself were sold away from father when I was quite small. I was there until colored people were freed. . . . All this time I never had a chance to go to school, for I had to work hard. . . . I used to watch the children every day as they went to school and wish that I could go.

"Mother learned me my alphabet and from that I learned to read the stories in the bible . . . [but] that was not all I wanted to know, so I asked the lady that I lived with if she wouldn't give me a lesson every night after I [finished] my work and she said she would. I was so glad I almost shouted with joy. During that time a nice new schoolhouse was built . . . for the colored children. . . . They had a splendid teacher, one of the Hampton Singers, Mr. Joseph Towe.

"... So with a very glad heart I put our home in order, cooked both breakfast and dinner early in the morning, then started for the very first time to school, a walk of two and a half miles. . . . I thought to myself sometimes I would have to give it up, but with the encouraging words of our teacher, Mr. Towe, every day made me forget the hard part and see only the good things I was learning. Hampton was talked up every week to us, at the close of the year everyone of us wanted to come.

"When I entered the preparatory class in 1877, there were only three hundred students—not half so many as now. [At Hampton, we] went to church service in the Little Bethesda Chapel. On Monday mornings between four and six, eight of us girls crept softly to do our own washing first, getting through it in time for the six o'clock breakfast, and after dishwashing reported to the laundry for our regular day's work. . . . I work a day out of school every week to help pay my board. . . . My chief desire is to get an education that I may be able to help my race. . . .

"In the latter part of this, my senior term, in 1882, a building was started near Virginia Hall for [American] Indian Girls. I was asked to remain at Hampton after graduating and assist in training [them] in their new home.

". . . It is said by some that two people down can't help each other, but we say here, two people rising together can help each other. Working side by side with another race helps us to grow large hearted, keeping ever before us Hampton's motto, 'Help one another.'"

—Georgia Washington, Hampton, Class of 1882

TOMATO, BLACK OLIVE, AND HOT PEPPER SALAD

2   green bell peppers
2   yellow bell peppers
1   cucumber, peeled, seeded, and diced
2   tablespoons diced onion
1   small fresh jalapeño pepper, seeded and minced

½   cup medium black olives, halved
    Salt and black pepper to taste
¼   cup lemon juice
3   garlic cloves, minced fine
¼   teaspoon ground cumin
¼   cup olive oil
¼   cup chopped cilantro

Char the peppers under a broiler, periodically turning them until they are charred on all sides. Quickly place the peppers into a plastic bag, and tightly seal the bag. Allow the peppers to cool. The steam created in the bag will facilitate removal of the charred skin. Once the peppers have cooled, remove them from the bag, remove the charred skin, rinse the peppers, pat them dry, and dice. Toss the vegetables together and add salt and pepper to taste. In a separate bowl, combine the lemon juice, garlic, cumin, and olive oil. Toss together with the vegetables. Just prior to serving, add the cilantro and toss well.

4 servings

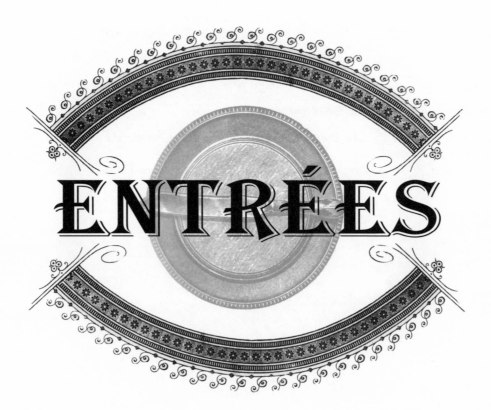

ENTRÉES

"In the early days of the Hampton School the great question agitating the Teacher's Home was not beefsteak or lamb chops, nor yet early dinner or late, but was simply how, by hook or crook, to secure enough food and ensure its being prepared as well as the poor material at hand would permit. They, like those who preceded them, turned to nature . . . the bounties of the ocean and of course the land."

—Alice M. Bacon, Hampton student and teacher, 1894

Roast Pheasant

1	3-pound pheasant	½	teaspoon black pepper
¼	cup (½ stick) softened butter	¼	teaspoon paprika
½	cup sherry	¼	teaspoon onion powder
1	teaspoon salt		

Preheat the oven to 350 degrees F. Wash the bird inside and out; pat dry. Combine the butter, 2 tablespoons of the sherry, and the seasonings. Place half of the remaining sherry in the cavity of the bird. Rub the seasoned butter inside and out. Tie the legs together with kitchen twine, tuck in the wings, and place the pheasant in a covered roasting pan. Pour the remaining sherry over the bird, cover, and bake, allowing 25 minutes per pound. Baste often with pan juices, adding additional sherry, if required. To test for doneness, press your finger into the flesh. If it's done, the flesh will spring back. If not, it will feel tight and firm. Allow to cool before serving.

4 to 6 servings

Roast Goose With Oyster Dressing and Sauce

Roast goose has become an increasingly popular holiday meal. Today's commercially produced geese have a thin layer of fat between the skin and the meat. This built-in "baster" keeps the dark meat moist throughout roasting.

	8- to 10-pound goose	½	teaspoon onion powder
½	lemon	½	teaspoon ground black pepper
2	teaspoons salt	3	16-ounce cans chicken broth
⅛	teaspoon garlic powder		

Preheat the oven to 400 degrees F. Remove any excess fat from the inside of the goose. Wash the goose thoroughly, inside and out, under running water. Dry the goose well and rub the inside with the lemon half. Combine the remaining ingredients and season the goose inside and out; then refrigerate while you prepare the Oyster Dressing (see below).

Once the dressing is prepared, remove the goose from the refrigerator. Spoon 1 cup of dressing into the neck cavity. Secure the neck flap with two or three poultry pins. Spoon the remaining dressing into the body cavity. Insert five poultry pins and use kitchen twine to lace the cavity closed, bootlace fashion. Fold the wing tips under the body. Next, twine the legs together.

Heat the broth and place it in the bottom of the roasting pan. Put the goose in the pan with the broth, breast side down. Roast uncovered for 50 minutes. Pour off the liquid from the pan and reserve for future use. Turn the goose breast side up. Place a rack beneath the goose; reduce the heat to 325 degrees. Roast uncovered for 20 minutes. With a fork, carefully prick the skin all over to release the fat from under the skin. Continue baking for 2½ hours. Prick twice more during the baking period. Place the goose on a warm serving platter and allow to stand for at least 20 minutes before attempting to carve. Pour off the drippings and degrease. Reserve the drippings for making gravy and sauces.

10 to 12 servings

OYSTER DRESSING

4 bacon strips	2 teaspoons salt
⅓ cup bacon drippings	¼ teaspoon ground black pepper
2 medium onions, chopped	1 pint oysters and their liquor
2 celery stalks, chopped	2 tablespoons chopped scallions,
1 loaf firm white bread, crumbled	including green tops

In a large skillet, fry the bacon until crisp, and remove to a paper towel to drain. Add to the skillet additional bacon drippings or oil as necessary to make ⅓ cup. Sauté the onions and celery in the drippings, until the onions become soft. Stir in the bread crumbs, then add salt and pepper. Transfer to a bowl. Drain the liquor from the oysters and reserve. Cut the oysters in half. Bring the reserved liquor to a boil. Reduce the heat to low; add the oysters and poach until their edges begin to curl. Drain and stir into the dressing, add the remaining ingredients, mix well, and use to stuff the goose.

OYSTER SAUCE

3	tablespoons minced onion	3	tablespoons heavy cream
2	tablespoons oil	1¼	teaspoons Worcestershire sauce
2	tablespoons flour	1	cup finely chopped oysters in their liquor
⅓	cup degreased goose drippings		Salt and ground white pepper to taste
1	cup milk		

Sauté the onion in oil over medium heat. Stir in the flour, then add the drippings. Whisk until smooth and add the milk, stirring constantly. Once the sauce begins to simmer, add the cream and Worcestershire sauce. Add additional drippings to thin, if necessary, or water if no drippings are available. Finally, add the oysters and salt and pepper to taste. Simmer until the oysters' edges begin to curl. Serve hot with roast goose.

How to Carve a Goose

1. Remove the wings and place on a warmed serving platter. With the legs facing you, hold the nearest leg and gently pull it away from the body. Cut through the skin and the leg joint. Remove the leg and place it on a cutting board. Repeat to remove the second leg.

2. With a sharp knife, cut down one side of the breastbone between the meat and the bone. Continue cutting to the wing joint, removing the breast meat with a fork. Place on a cutting board. Repeat to remove remaining breast meat.

3. Hold the breast meat on board or platter and slice diagonally.

4. To remove the meat from the legs, hold the leg bone and cut toward the end of the bone, loosening the meat; slice the meat.

ROAST GOOSE WITH PLUM SAUCE AND SAGE DRESSING

8- to 10-pound goose	½ teaspoon onion powder
½ lemon	¼ teaspoon ground sage
2 tablespoons salt	½ teaspoon black pepper
⅛ teaspoon garlic powder	3 16-ounce cans chicken broth

Preheat the oven to 400 degrees F. Remove any excess fat from the inside of the goose. Wash the goose thoroughly, inside and out, under running water. Dry the goose well and rub the inside with the lemon half. Combine the next five dry seasoning ingredients and season the goose inside and out; then refrigerate while you prepare the Sage Dressing (below).

Once the dressing is prepared, remove the goose from the refrigerator. Spoon 1 cup of dressing into the neck cavity. Secure the neck flap with two or three poultry pins. Spoon the remaining dressing into the body cavity. Insert five poultry pins and use kitchen twine to lace the cavity closed, bootlace fashion. Fold the wing tips under the body. Then twine the legs together.

Heat the broth and place it in the bottom of the roasting pan. Put the goose in the pan with the broth, breast side down. Roast uncovered for 50 minutes. Pour off the liquid from the pan and reserve for future use. Turn the goose breast side up. Place a rack beneath the goose; reduce the heat to 325 degrees. Roast uncovered for 20 minutes. With a fork, carefully prick the skin all over to release fat from under the skin. Continue baking for 2½ hours. Prick twice more during the baking period. Place the goose on a warm serving platter and allow to stand for at least 20 minutes before attempting to carve. Pour off the drippings and degrease. Reserve the drippings for making gravy and sauces.

10 to 12 servings

SAGE DRESSING

¼ cup bacon drippings	½ teaspoon ground black pepper
3 large onions, chopped	⅛ teaspoon celery seeds
1 green bell pepper, chopped	1½ tablespoons dried sage
8 cups lightly toasted bread cubes	1½ teaspoons poultry seasoning
¾ teaspoon seasoned salt	¾ teaspoon onion powder
	½ teaspoon garlic powder

In a large, heavy skillet, heat the drippings over medium-high heat and sauté the onions and bell pepper until the onions are soft. Transfer to a bowl and combine with the remaining ingredients. Mix well and use to stuff the goose.

PLUM SAUCE

1 pound damson plums	Pinch (¹⁄₁₆ teaspoon) of ground allspice
3 cups water	Pinch of cayenne pepper
1 cup port	1 tablespoon cornstarch
⅓ cup degreased pan drippings	2 tablespoons water
2 teaspoons sugar	
⅛ teaspoon ground cinnamon	

Wash and pit the plums. Bring the 3 cups of water to a boil and add the plums; bring it to a second boil and simmer until the plums are tender, 20 to 30 minutes. Remove from the heat and set aside. In a medium saucepan, over low heat, simmer the port, uncovered, until reduced to ½ cup. Add the drippings and cook for 5 minutes. Drain the plums, crush them slightly with a fork, and add to port mixture along with the sugar, seasonings and spices. Simmer for 5 minutes. In a separate container, mix together the cornstarch with 2 tablespoons water and stir to form a paste. Add to the plum mixture. Bring to a quick boil and continue to cook, stirring occasionally, until the sauce is translucent, about 20 minutes. Serve with goose.

Zimbabwe Pheasant

2   pheasants, prepared and
    disjointed
1   bottle red wine
2   tablespoons dried thyme
    Salt and black pepper to taste
1   cup flour
1   teaspoon salt
¼   teaspoon ground black
    pepper

½   teaspoon onion powder
2   tablespoons dried thyme
5   pieces thick-sliced Canadian bacon
2   large onions, sliced thin
3   tablespoons whipping cream
2   tablespoons red currant jelly
    Chopped fresh parsley, for garnish

Wash the pheasant pieces under cold running water and set aside to drain. Combine the wine and thyme in a nonreactive pan, and marinate pheasants overnight. The next day, drain the wine into a container and reserve. Lightly season the pheasant with salt and pepper. Combine the flour and remaining seasoning ingredients. Flour the pheasant pieces and set aside. In a large, deep casserole, fry the bacon until crisp and set the bacon aside. Sauté the pheasant in the bacon drippings. Add the onions and sauté until soft. Add the reserved marinade to the pan and heat gently, scraping sediment from the bottom and sides of the pan. Crumble the bacon into casserole. Cover and cook over low heat for 2½ hours. Remove the cover for the last half hour of cooking. Before serving, stir in the cream and red currant jelly. Garnish with fresh-chopped parsley. Serve with nutty wild rice.

8 servings

Cidah press commence a-squeakin',

Eatin' apples sto'ed away,

Chillun swa'min 'roun' lak ho'nets,

Huntin' aigs emung de hay.

At de geese a-flyin' souf,

Oomph: dat bird do' know whut's comin';

Ef he don shet his mouf. . . .

Tu'key gobbler gwine 'roun' blowin',

Gwine 'roun' gibbin sass an' slack;

Keep on talkin', Mistah Tu'key

You ain't seed no almanac. . . .

Look heyeah, Turkey stop dat gobblin',

You ain' luned de sense ob feah

You ol' fool yo' naik's in dangah,

Do' you know Thanksgibbin's hyeah?

—Excerpted from *Signs of the Times*
by Paul Laurence Dunbar

ROAST TURKEY AND GIBLET GRAVY

As I write this in the middle of August, I am already anticipating the holiday season, which would not be complete in our home without mouthwatering roasted turkey.

	18- to 24-pound turkey with neck and giblets	2	teaspoons dried thyme
1½	teaspoons garlic powder	1	large onion, quartered
1½	teaspoons onion powder	1	green bell pepper, seeded and quartered
1½	teaspoons ground black pepper	1	navel orange, quartered
1½	teaspoons salt	1	apple, seeded and quartered
2	teaspoons meat tenderizer	2	celery stalks with leaves, halved
1	tablespoon poultry seasoning	1	cup orange juice
1	teaspoon ground sage	¼	cup lime juice

Preheat the oven to 325 degrees F. Remove the giblets and neck from turkey cavity, and rinse the removed parts and the bird under cold running water. Pat the bird dry, then place it breast side up in a roasting pan. Mix together the dry ingredients and thoroughly season the bird, inside and out, with the mixture. Don't forget the neck cavity. Fill the neck and body cavity with the cut-up fruit and vegetables. Combine the orange and lime juices, and pour into the body cavity. Fold the wings under the body and truss the legs. Cover the breast with a piece of aluminum foil and roast for 15 minutes per pound. Baste every 30 minutes and remove the foil after approximately 1 hour to allow the bird to brown. Check often, and replace the foil if the bird is browning too fast. Serve with dressing, Giblet Gravy (below), sweet potato casserole, fresh collard greens, Homemade Cranberry Cups (see page 166), and yeast rolls.

12 to 18 servings

GIBLET GRAVY

5	cups chicken stock	½	cup chopped green bell pepper
	Turkey giblets and neck	2	tablespoons bacon drippings or lard
½	pound chicken giblets	1	cup milk
½	cup chopped yellow onion	¼	cup flour
¼	cup chopped celery		

In a medium saucepan, bring the chicken stock to boil, and add the washed turkey and chicken giblets. Reduce the heat and simmer for 30 to 45 minutes. In a separate pan, sauté the onion, celery, and green pepper in bacon drippings until the onion is almost transparent. Stir to prevent sticking. Set aside. After removing the cooked turkey from the pan to a serving platter, place the meat pan over two burners and deglaze with reserved giblet juice. After deglazing, place the drippings in a medium pot, add the milk, and cook over medium heat. Next, add the vegetables and chopped giblets. Finally, add the flour and stir constantly with a wire whisk until the gravy reaches the desired consistency. Use additional flour paste or milk to adjust the consistency. Serve with roast turkey and Southern Corn Bread Dressing (page 159).

The cheese press screw: students studying agricultural sciences.
(Reproduced from the collections of the Library of Congress)

Duck come switchin' 'cross de lot

Hi, oh Miss Lady!

Hurry up and hide de pot

Hi, oh, Miss Lady! . . .

Ain't he fat and ain't he fine,

Hi, oh, Miss Lady!

Des can't wait to make him mine.

Hi, oh Miss Lady!

—Excerpted from *The Capture*
by Paul Laurence Dunbar

ROAST DUCK WITH ORANGE SAUCE

1   5-pound duck, plucked,
     prepped, and cleaned
6   tablespoons cognac, divided
1   tablespoon salt
½   teaspoon freshly ground black
     pepper
1   teaspoon ground thyme
1   medium onion, quartered

½   inch fresh ginger, sliced into
     10 pieces
1   orange, quartered
1   bay leaf
1   medium sweet potato, uncooked,
     pierced several times
2   tablespoons butter

Wash the duck with cold water. Prick the skin around the thighs, back, and over the breast to allow fat to escape during cooking. Dry completely and rub the duck inside and out with 3 tablespoons of the cognac. Place an additional tablespoon of cognac inside the bird and shake. Rub salt inside the duck. Rub additional cognac on the outside of the duck and sprinkle with salt, rubbing salt into the skin (don't forget the area under the neck skin). Cover the duck and refrigerate overnight.

Remove the duck from the refrigerator and allow to stand at room temperature for 7 to 8 hours before it is to be cooked (this allows the skin to dry, for a crispier result when roasted). Preheat the oven to 350 degrees F. Season the bird inside and out with the pepper and thyme. Place three-quarters of the onion, five pieces of the ginger, the orange, and the bay leaf in the cavity of the bird. Add the remaining ginger and sliced onion under the neck skin. Stretch the neck skin over the sweet potato. Attach to the duck with two or more skewers. Rub the outside of the duck with butter, then season with additional black pepper and thyme. Roast uncovered for half an hour. The potato absorbs excess fat and basting liquid during cooking. Reduce the heat to 250 degrees and continue to roast, uncovered, for an additional 2 hours. Drain the fat from the pan. Return the duck to the oven and increase the heat to 410 degrees. Cook for an additional 30 minutes. Check often to ensure the duck does not become too brown. If it is browning too fast, cover the roaster loosely with foil. Place the duck on a warm platter to keep warm.

4 to 6 servings

ORANGE SAUCE

½	cup sugar		¼	cup unsalted chicken broth
½	cup vinegar		¼	cup orange peel (remove bitter white
	Juice of 2 oranges			part and cut peel into strips
	Grated rind of 1 orange			⅛ inch wide)
½	cup Madeira			

Degrease the pan drippings. Bring the sugar and vinegar to a boil in a heavy saucepan over medium heat; add the orange juice, grated orange rind, and Madeira. Reduce the heat and simmer over low heat for 15 minutes. Deglaze the roasting pan with broth and add to orange sauce. Add the orange strips, simmer 3 minutes, pour over the warm duck, and serve.

HONEY-PEACH-GLAZED DUCK

1	5-pound duck, washed and quartered	⅓	cup apricot preserves
2	ripe unpeeled peaches, pitted	1½	tablespoons brandy
1	¾-inch piece of fresh ginger, peeled	¼	cup honey
2	large garlic cloves	1	teaspoon salt
		1	orange, peeled and quartered

Refrigerate the prepared duck. In a food processor, purée the peaches, ginger, and garlic. Add the preserves, brandy, and honey. Process until smooth. Reserve half the purée. Place the remainder in a large plastic bag with the duck. Seal the bag tightly and refrigerate for a minimum of 2 hours, or preferably overnight. Turn occasionally. Preheat the oven to 325 degrees F. Place the duck, skin side up, on a rack in a baking dish. Bake for 1 hour. Drain the fat and arrange duck in baking dish. Sprinkle with salt. Brush the duck with the reserved purée. Add the orange slices, cover, and bake for an additional 30 to 40 minutes. Cook for the last 10 minutes uncovered. Excellent when grilled over mesquite chips.

4 servings

I learned to love quail as a young girl in my grandmother's kitchen. My grandfather enjoyed hunting and on Sundays, after a hunt, he would rise early, light the kerosene heaters, and prepare breakfast before we went to church. My cousin and I, wrapped in warm winter robes, with freshly pressed and curled hair, would rush to the breakfast table having been teased by the delicious kitchen smells all morning.

My favorite breakfast was always his smothered quail accompanied by grits and, on occasion, a fluffy, fat hoe-cake (a southern pancake) drenched in delicious butter and cane syrup. Those Sundays, in which the aroma of fresh coffee filled the kitchen and bright beams of winter sunshine spilled across the breakfast table, are among my most treasured childhood memories. I truly hope you will enjoy the recipes, which follow.

ROASTED VIRGINIA QUAIL WITH GRAPE SAUCE

4	oven-ready quail
	Salt and black pepper to taste
6	tablespoons butter
40	seedless white grapes, halved
	Bacon drippings
¼	cup cognac, divided
4	hickory-smoked bacon strips, blanched
1	tablespoon vegetable oil
2	large garlic cloves, minced
7	shallots, finely chopped
½	pound Virginia ham, cut into 2- by 1-inch strips
¾	cup dry sherry
⅛	teaspoon grated ginger
1	cup chicken stock
1½	teaspoons cornstarch
1	teaspoon orange zest
1	tablespoon fresh orange juice
	Degreased pan juices

Preheat the oven to 400 degrees F. Wash the quail and pat dry. Salt and pepper each cavity to taste and then fill with ½ tablespoon butter and eight grape halves. Rub the outside of each bird with bacon drippings and sprinkle with additional salt and pepper to taste. Sprinkle with cognac. Top each breast with a slice of bacon. Place the quail on a rack in a shallow roasting pan. Bake for 15 or 20 minutes. Baste with 3 tablespoons of the butter, 1 tablespoon vegetable oil, and 1 teaspoon cognac. Test for doneness (when pricked, juices should run clear). When almost done, remove the bacon, baste, and brown the quail under a broiler. Remove to a heated serving platter. Sauté the garlic and shallots in 2 tablespoons butter. When the shallots are soft, add the ham. Next, in a separate container, mix together the sherry, ginger, stock, and cornstarch. Add the sherry mixture to the pan; stir in the orange zest, orange juice, and degreased pan juices. Stir well, scraping any brown bits from the bottom of the pan. Simmer until slightly thickened. If it's too thick, add water. Add the remaining grapes, simmer for 5 additional minutes, and pour the sauce over the quail. Serve immediately.

4 servings

SAUTÉED QUAIL

4	oven-ready quail	3	tablespoons cognac
6	tablespoons butter	1	cup large seedless red grapes
16	juniper berries		Salt and black pepper to taste
½	cup dry white wine		

Wash the quail under cold running water, place in a colander, and set aside to drain. Melt 3 tablespoons of the butter in a casserole; place four juniper berries inside each quail and sauté for a few minutes. Add the wine, cover, and simmer gently for 15 minutes. Add the cognac and flambé while shaking the casserole. Add the grapes and simmer for another 10 or 15 minutes. Season with salt and pepper to taste and serve immediately with Wild Rice Timbales (p. 170).

4 servings

ROAST CHICKEN WITH GRAVY

You'll laugh, you'll cry—you will pass your plates for a second helping. Words are simply inadequate to describe this delicious dish!

1	3-pound roasting chicken	2	celery stalks, halved
1	lemon, halved	2	small garlic cloves
1	tablespoon seasoned salt	1	large onion, quartered
2	teaspoons onion powder	1	large green bell pepper, seeded and quartered
1	teaspoon garlic powder		
½	teaspoon poultry seasoning	4	tablespoons cold butter
1	teaspoon crushed rosemary	1	16-ounce can chicken broth

Preheat the oven to 375 degrees F. Thoroughly wash, rinse, and pat the chicken dry. Rub it inside and out with the lemon and its juice. Combine the next five seasoning ingredients. Season the chicken to taste by rubbing this mixture inside and out. Stuff with the celery, garlic, onions, and bell pepper. Place four 1-tablespoon slices of butter throughout the cavity. Bake for 1½ hours, basting periodically. Add some chicken broth if required.

6 servings

GRAVY

Flour

Remove the chicken to a warm platter and keep warm. Drain the drippings and degrease. Place the drippings into a medium saucepan. Add the remaining broth and stir. Remove ½ cup of liquid from the saucepan. Stir 2 tablespoons of flour into the liquid; return the mixture to the pot, and cook over medium-high heat, stirring frequently, until the mixture begins to thicken. Repeat the process as necessary to reach the desired consistency. If the gravy is too thick, add broth or water as desired.

ROAST LEG OF LAMB

1	6-pound trimmed leg of lamb	¼	teaspoon garlic powder
¼	cup water	¼	teaspoon cayenne pepper
¼	cup fresh lemon juice	¼	teaspoon paprika
1	teaspoon lemon zest	½	teaspoon lemon pepper
7	garlic cloves, halved		Freshly ground black pepper
2	tablespoons olive oil	1	tablespoon dried rosemary, crushed
2	teaspoons seasoned salt	1	tablespoon ground thyme
1	teaspoon onion powder		

Place the lamb in a nonreactive baking dish. Prepare the lamb by making fourteen 1-inch-deep pockets in its surface—seven on each side. Space the pockets evenly. Next, combine the water, lemon juice, and lemon zest; pour this mixture over the lamb. Insert half a garlic clove in each pocket. Rub the lamb with oil; combine the remaining seasoning ingredients and rub into both sides of the lamb.

Cover the pan with foil and allow the lamb to stand for 2 hours before roasting. Without removing the foil, place the lamb in an oven preheated to 350 degrees F.; roast, covered, for 1 hour. Remove the foil and roast for an additional 1½ hours, or until the meat reaches an internal temperature of 175 to 180 degrees. Baste frequently with pan drippings.

Allow to stand for 10 minutes before attempting to carve. Slice thin and pour warm, degreased pan drippings over the lamb before serving.

10 to 12 servings

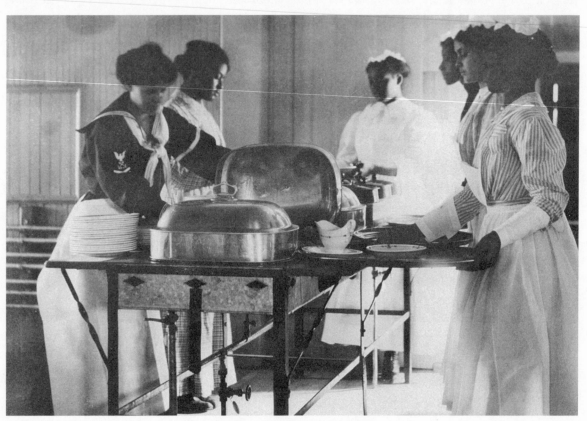

Holly Tree kitchen 1911
(Courtesy of Hampton University Archives)

Trouble in de Kitchen

by Paul Laurence Dunbar

Dey was oncet a awful quoil 'twixt de skillet an' de pot;

De pot was des a-bilin' an' de skillet sho' was hot.

Dey slurred each otha's colah an' dey called each othah names,

W'ile de coal-oil can des gu-gled poin oil erpon de flames.

De pot, hit called de skillet des a flat disfiggered t'ing,

An' de skillet plied dat all de pot could do was set an' sing,

An' he 'lowed dat dey was 'lusions dat he wouldn't stoop to mek

'Case he rekernize his juty, and he had too much at steak.

Well, at dis de pot biled ovah, case his tempah gittin' highah,

An de skillet got to sputterin', den de fat was in de fiah.

Mistah fiah lay daih smokin' an' a-t'inkin' to hisself,

W'ile de peppah-box us nudgin' of de gingah on de she'f.

Den dey all des lef' hit to 'im, bout de trouble an' de talk;

An' howevah he decided, w'y dey bofe 'u'd walf de chalk;

But de fiah uz so 'sgusted how dey quoil an' de shout

Dat he cooled 'em off, I reckon, w'en he puffed an' des went out.

ROAST PORK WITH SWEET POTATOES AND APPLES

	5-pound pork loin roast	⅛	teaspoon ground cloves
3	tablespoons vegetable oil	2	medium onions, sliced
1½	teaspoons salt	3	sweet potatoes (about 2 pounds), halved
1	teaspoon onion powder		
¼	teaspoon ground allspice	1	teaspoon ground cinnamon
⅛	teaspoon ground nutmeg	¼	teaspoon ground nutmeg
½	teaspoon ground black pepper	⅓	cup light brown sugar
		6	tart, firm red apples, cored

Preheat the oven to 350 degrees F. Wash the roast, pat it dry, and pierce it in several places with a two-prong fork. Rub the roast with the oil. Then combine the next six seasoning ingredients and rub them into the roast. Place the onions on the bottom of a large roasting pan. Place the roast in the pan, fat side down. Roast for 35 minutes per pound. Allow the roast to cook undisturbed for 2 hours, then arrange the halved sweet potatoes around it and roast for an additional 15 minutes. Combine the cinnamon, nutmeg, and brown sugar, and pack the cored apples with this mixture. Remove the roast from the oven and place the apples around it by alternating them with the potatoes. Return the roast to the oven and roast for an additional 35 minutes or until it reaches an internal temperature of 165 degrees.

10 servings

ROAST PORK IN PEACH SAUCE

	5-pound pork loin roast	¼	teaspoon ground allspice
3	garlic cloves, quartered	½	teaspoon ground black pepper
3	tablespoons vegetable oil	⅛	teaspoon ground cloves
1½	teaspoons salt	2	medium onions, sliced
1	teaspoon onion powder	4	bay leaves

Wash the roast, pat it dry, and pierce it in several places with a two prong fork. Force a garlic quarter into each hole. If necessary, use a paring knife to widen the hole. Rub the roast with vegetable oil and set aside. Mix together the next five seasoning ingredients and rub them into the roast. Refrigerate for up to 3 hours or, if possible, overnight. Preheat the oven to 325 degrees F. Combine the Spiced Peach Syrup ingredients (see below) and set aside. Place the onions and bay leaves in the bottom of a roasting pan. Place the roast in the pan, fat side down. Roast the pork loin, allowing 35 minutes cooking time per pound. Baste occasionally with Spiced Peach Syrup. During the last 15 to 20 minutes of cooking time, cover the roast with peaches (see Spiced Peach Syrup recipe below), attaching them with toothpicks.

8 to 10 servings

SPICED PEACH SYRUP

1	large can peach halves in heavy syrup	½	teaspoon ground cinnamon
½	teaspoon ground allspice	⅛	teaspoon ground cloves

Combine the peaches and syrup with the remaining ingredients, and use to baste the roast according to the above directions.

New Students Arrive

The first American Indian students arrived in Hampton on April 13, 1878. Captured during the Indian Wars, they were imprisoned at Old Fort Marion in St. Augustine, Florida, until the federal government no longer considered them "dangerous." Upon their release they were offered the option of returning to their homes in the west or continuing their education in the east.

"The arrival of these new [American] Indian students was a dramatic scene as they disembarked in the middle of the night from the steamer bringing them from Florida . . . the school quickly rushed to receive them, . . . with welcome and hot coffee . . . the two large recitation rooms were given up to them."

—Helen W. Ludlow

Eventually, as Hampton's American Indian education program continued to grow, two dormitories for the students were completed in 1882—The Wigwam for boys and Winona for girls. And graduate Hampton students such as Georgia Washington and Booker T. Washington (no relation) were selected as residential leaders to assist with the educational needs of these new students. The American Indian education program at Hampton, much like the program developed for African-American students provided a structured program which trained, "the head, the hand and the heart." Thus the program combined academic course work, manual training and Christian course work to provide an "education for life."

". . . In the fall of 1882 I began as a helper in Winona lodge, a ten years work for a people similar in many ways to my own, yet in others so different. The girls did not understand English and I did not understand Indian so we had an interpreter and used sign language which was very practical. . . ."

—Georgia Washington, Hampton, Class of 1882

". . . As part of the manual training aspect of the program, [American Indian] "girls are taught to mend, cut and make their own dresses, to sew by hand and machine, to wash and iron their own clothes. . . ."

—Helen W. Ludlow, Hampton teacher

"... I had two classes in laundry work in the morning and two in the afternoon. . . . Because they did not understand English, getting the names of the pieces of clothes was hard at first. . . . Having just finished school I was full of theory and practice of teaching. Practice lived, but theory died a natural death. The [American] Indian girls at first, would try ironing with a half hot flat iron and it would stick to the clothes, and the cold iron, instead of going back on the stove, often landed decidedly in the back of the room. . . . Sometimes as we stood side by side working away at the same piece of clothes, my wonder was which way the iron would go next. With week in and week out practice [the American Indian girls] made marked improvement. . . ."

—Georgia Washington

The American Indian Program at Hampton Prospers

The American Indian Program at Hampton continued to prosper and the Hampton system, which provided an "education for life," produced strong leaders, and became a model for other programs such as the one at Carlisle Barracks in Pennsylvania. Among those in the first class, arriving with Captain Pratt, were James Bears Heart, who learned carpentry, art, and pottery and became a major artist. Other prominent artists to arrive with this first group include Ethahdleau Doanmoe, Koba, and William Kohoe.

Susan La Flesche Picotte graduated as salutatorian of the class of 1886. The daughter of an Omaha Chief, she entered the Women's Medical College in 1889 and became the first American Indian to receive a medical degree. Manual training at Hampton continued as well. Georgia Washington would later recall: "... [a] pleasanter work entrusted to me was the cooking and housekeeping instruction in the . . . housekeeping cottage. . . . Four afternoons every week, three [American Indian] girls go up to a small cottage on the grounds and prepare their supper. The school gives us all the milk, flour and meal we need so the allowance money goes to buy meat, eggs or anything wanted for the suppers. . . ."

—*Hampton and Its Students*

American Indian Students Dedicate Themselves to Service

American Indian students were also encouraged to organize their own socials and clubs. Combined meetings of the American Indian students were encouraged and, as Helen Ludlow would later write, were held in, "Winona Lodge, where the girls and their teachers act as hostesses. Here are held the Lend-a-Hand Clubs, which sent last year a Christmas box to each Indian girl who is teaching. . . ."

At Hampton, service to society was emphasized with the goal of producing graduates who return to their communities and become leaders of their people. "[The] test of work was not what the [American Indian] students received at the school, but rather their record on their return home. . . . The work to be done is yet at the reservation."

—General Samuel C. Armstrong, Hampton Founder and First Principal

The "record" of these Hampton graduates work on the reservation was often contained in letters to teachers and friends who remained at Hampton.

"Dear Miss Ludlow:
    . . . You are familiar with the story of those Hampton students . . . Philip and Lucy La Flesch. Two years ago their lands were unbroken prairie. To-day they have nearly . . . fifty acres and expect to break more this spring. . . ."

—Miss Alice C. Fletcher Winnebago Agency, Neb., February 8, 1888

These Hampton graduates took their lessons home with them, setting an example for others to follow. Lucy La Flesch would write, "After breakfast when my rooms are in order, I sit down to sew. I have shirts and pillowslips to make and table cloths and napkins to hem."

The "record" is also clear that they mastered the ironing lessons taught by Hampton Industrial Teacher, Georgia Washington, which they enjoyed sharing with those at home. In doing so they emulated Miss Washington's example as they began to "help one another." Not only did Hampton graduates set the example, but they also rolled up their sleeves and helped. ". . . I go over to help Rosalie wash every other week. I love to help her. I helped Susette wash too. . . . When their washing day comes, they come over after me. I have strong arms so I am willing to help them. . . ."

—Lucy La Flesch, Hampton Graduate

Students painting watercolor picture of butterflies
(Reproduced from the collections of the Library of Congress)

The American Indian students also wrote of their great love for their alma mater. Miss J.E.B. wrote, "Please give my love to all the girls in Winona. I think of them all at Hampton and I am proud when People ask me where I went to school."

—J.E.B., New Haven, Conn. January 8, 1888

VIRGINIA HAM AND BRANDIED PEACHES

	10- to 12-pound Virginia ham	½	teaspoon ground allspice
3	tablespoons light brown sugar	⅛	teaspoon ground cinnamon
1	teaspoon dry mustard	1	tablespoon molasses
1	tablespoon fine bread crumbs	3	tablespoons honey
1	teaspoon ground cloves	1	tablespoon dry sherry
			Brandied Peaches (see page 200)

Cover the ham with cold water and soak for 24 to 36 hours before cooking. Using a stiff brush, scrub away the mold from the ham's surface. Cover the ham with fresh cold water. Slowly simmer for 20 to 25 minutes per pound, or until the ham reaches an internal temperature of 150 degrees F. When cooking is complete, drain the liquid from the ham and discard. Remove the skin from the ham while it is still warm, leaving the fat intact. Trim away any excess fat and score the remaining fat into diamond shapes.

Preheat the oven to 375 degrees F. Combine the brown sugar, dry mustard, bread crumbs, and spices. Press the mixture into the scored ham. Place the ham in a shallow baking pan and bake for 15 minutes, until the sugar melts. Combine the molasses, honey, and sherry. Remove the ham from the oven and drizzle the molasses mixture over it; return it to the oven for an additional 15 minutes.

Serve garnished with Brandied Peaches and spiced crab apples.

12 to 16 servings

FRIED HAM WITH REDEYE GRAVY

4 slices cured or country ham, ¼ to ½ inch thick	½ cup hot water
3 tablespoons hot coffee	

Gash the fat around the ham's edges to prevent them from curling while cooking. If the ham is very salty, cover with water and simmer briefly, turning frequently. Discard the water and continue to fry in a cast-iron or other heavy skillet over moderate heat, turning several times until brown on each side. Once done, remove from the pan and keep warm. There should be a reddish brown glaze on the bottom of the pan. Add hot coffee and water to the pan while stirring and cooking until the gravy turns red. Serve with grits, redeye gravy, and hot Buttermilk Biscuits (page 180).

4 servings

Students are taught mathematic geography
(Reproduced from the collections of the Library of Congress)

HERBED RABBIT IN PORT SAUCE

1	rabbit, dressed and disjointed			Flour
2	sprigs fresh thyme		¼	cup vegetable oil
1	sprig fresh rosemary		¾	cup chopped shallots
1	small bay leaf		2	garlic cloves, minced
2	tablespoons juniper berries		1½	cups ruby port
2	cups buttermilk		1½	cups chicken broth
	Salt and black pepper			

Wash the rabbit, pat dry, and place in a bowl with the herb sprigs, bay leaf, and juniper berries. Pour the buttermilk over the rabbit, cover, and refrigerate overnight. Remove the rabbit from the marinade and pat dry. Season the rabbit with salt and pepper, and flour lightly. In a large skillet, heat the vegetable oil over high heat. When a drop of water can dance across the surface of the oil, add the rabbit, one piece at a time. Do not crowd the pan. Sauté until browned, turning once, about 3 minutes on each side. Remove the rabbit to a baking dish and keep warm. Remove all but 2 tablespoons of oil from the pan; stir in the shallots and garlic. Sauté until the shallots are soft, about 2 minutes. Add the port and chicken stock. Bring to a boil, reduce the heat, and simmer for 5 minutes. Pour the hot mixture over the rabbit. Cover the rabbit and bake until fork-tender, about 35 to 40 minutes. Degrease the sauce and thin with additional chicken broth, if necessary.

4 servings

BRAISED RABBIT

1	rabbit, dressed and disjointed		¼	teaspoon thyme
	Salt and black pepper to taste		⅛	teaspoon crushed rosemary
1¼	cups flour		½	cup chopped onion
1	teaspoon salt		¼	cup bacon drippings or shortening
1¼	teaspoons ground black pepper			Water

Wash the rabbit and pat dry. Salt and pepper the rabbit pieces to taste. Combine the flour, salt, pepper, thyme, and rosemary. Dredge the rabbit in the flour mixture, then refrigerate the seasoned rabbit while you chop the onion. In a heavy skillet, heat the bacon drippings over medium-high heat. Remove the rabbit from the refrigerator and brown on all sides in the hot drippings. Remove the browned rabbit pieces from the pan and allow to drain on a paper-towel-covered plate. Set aside and keep warm. Add the onion to the pan and sauté until it's transparent. Return the rabbit to the pan, add water to barely cover rabbit pieces, cover pan tightly, and simmer over low heat until tender, approximately 1½ hours. Serve for breakfast with grits and hot biscuits or for dinner with steamed rice, yams, and hot biscuits.

4 servings

Dairy class demonstration of milk testing
(Reproduced from the collections of the Library of Congress)

Students are taught methods of creaming
(Reproduced from the collections of the Library of Congress)

FRIED FROG LEGS IN CREAM SAUCE

8	pairs large skinned frog legs
	Salt and black pepper to taste
½	cup flour
1	teaspoon salt
¼	teaspoon paprika

⅛	teaspoon cayenne pepper
⅛	teaspoon garlic powder
½	teaspoon onion powder
¼	cup (½ stick) butter
¼	cup vegetable oil

Wash the legs and soak them in salted water for 15 minutes (1 tablespoon salt per 2 quarts water). Thoroughly drain the legs, add salt and pepper to taste, and set aside. Combine the flour and the next five seasoning ingredients in a plastic bag. Flour the legs, one pair at a time, and place on a platter.

In a large, heavy skillet, melt the butter over medium-high heat. Reduce the heat to medium and add the frog legs. Fry for approximately 8 to 10 minutes on each side or until the legs are brown and tender when pierced with a fork. Drain on absorbent paper and keep warm while preparing cream sauce.

2 to 4 servings

CREAM SAUCE

2½ tablespoons pan drippings
   (from previous recipe)
2 tablespoons flour
1 cup half-and-half

¼ teaspoon salt
⅛ teaspoon white pepper
1½ teaspoons minced chives

Remove all but 2½ tablespoons of drippings from the skillet in which the frog legs were fried. Brown the flour in the drippings for 2 or 3 minutes. Add the remaining ingredients. Stir constantly over medium-high heat until the mixture reaches the desired consistency. If necessary, thin with additional half-and-half. Serve with hot frog legs.

4 servings

PAN-FRIED RABBIT

1 3-pound rabbit, dressed and
   disjointed
Salt and black pepper to taste
⅓ cup all-purpose flour
¼ teaspoon seasoned salt
½ teaspoon dry mustard
¼ teaspoon fresh-ground black
   pepper
¼ teaspoon paprika
⅛ teaspoon cayenne pepper

1 teaspoon brown sugar
3 tablespoons shortening
3 tablespoons bacon drippings
½ cup chopped onion
2 tablespoons tomato paste
2 cans beef bouillon
¼ cup port
2 tablespoons red wine
2 tablespoons currant jelly

Wash the rabbit pieces and pat dry. Lightly salt and pepper to taste. Combine the flour with the next six seasoning ingredients and dredge the rabbit pieces in this mixture to coat. In a heavy skillet, heat the shortening and bacon drippings, add the rabbit pieces, and brown on all sides. Cook for 5 to 7 minutes on both sides over moderate heat. Remove the browned rabbit pieces from the pan and allow to drain on a paper-towel-covered plate. Set aside and keep warm.

Drain all but 3 tablespoons of oil from the pan or add additional oil to make 3 tablespoons. Sauté the onion until transparent. Add the flour that you used to dredge the rabbit, stirring constantly until the flour reaches a deep, rich brown color. Remove the pan from the heat. Blend in the tomato paste. Add the bouillon and stir until smooth. Return the rabbit pieces to the pan, adding additional beef bouillon or water sufficient to cover them.

Reduce the heat to low; cover and simmer for 1½ to 2 hours or until fork-tender. Remove the rabbit to a warm platter and keep warm while continuing to cook the sauce over medium heat for an additional 10 minutes. Stir constantly until sauce reaches the desired consistency. Add the port, red wine, and jelly. Pour over the rabbit and serve hot.

4 servings

Serving dinner
(Courtesy of Hampton University Archives)

Student cooking an omelet
(Courtesy of Hampton University Archives)

OLD BAY SEAFOOD SEASONING

1	tablespoon ground bay leaves		1½	teaspoons ground black pepper
2	tablespoons celery salt		1	teaspoon cayenne pepper
1½	teaspoons garlic powder		1½	teaspoons paprika
1	teaspoon onion powder		¾	teaspoon ground cloves
¼	teaspoon ground allspice		1	teaspoon ground nutmeg
1	teaspoon dry mustard		1	teaspoon dried oregano
¼	teaspoon curry powder		1	teaspoon dried thyme

Combine the above ingredients, mix well, and store in an airtight container. Use in stews, soups, gumbos, and, of course, to season seafood.

Cleaning Fish

"When I came to Hampton in 1871 . . . [the] Old Barracks, a long wooden one story building was used as a girl's quarters, and also contained the student's kitchen and dining room. —My second days work—and a good many more—was cleaning fish to help 'Uncle Tom,' the cook. I thought that much worse than pulling corn. I had five dollars where I could get it, for I thought I should be compelled to walk home, I did so hate to clean fish."

—Hampton student

PLANKED SHAD

The freshness of seafood can be judged by its appearance and odor. Fresh fish have full, clear eyes, red gills, and shiny skin with glistening color. Additionally, the skin should spring back when touched. It should have either no odor or a mild odor. Store in the coldest part of your refrigerator. Fresh fish is best when used within one or two days of purchase. Freeze for longer storage.

1	4-pound shad, split and boned, with head and tail intact	½	teaspoon salt
		¼	teaspoon black pepper
			Pinch (1/16 teaspoon) of nutmeg
2	tablespoons sherry	¼	teaspoon cayenne pepper

Prepare a plank according to manufacturer's directions or by thoroughly oiling an untreated hardwood plank and placing it in a cold oven. Turn the oven to 400 degrees F. and allow the plank to heat for approximately 15 minutes. While the plank is heating, wash the shad, pat it dry, then rub it inside and out with the sherry. Combine the salt and spices and rub the mixture into the fish. Place the shad on the hot plank; place a drip pan beneath the plank; reduce the heat to 375 degrees and bake, allowing 10 to 15 minutes per pound.

4 servings

SHRIMP- AND CRAB-STUFFED SHAD

1	4- to 5-pound shad, split and boned, with head and tail intact	3	bacon slices, minced
		½	cup finely chopped onion
5	tablespoons butter	3	green onions, sliced thin, including tops
5	tablespoons sherry	¾	cup finely chopped celery
1	teaspoon salt	1	cup small shrimp
½	teaspoon paprika	1	cup lump crabmeat
½	teaspoon ground white pepper	1	cup bread crumbs
		2	eggs, well beaten
⅛	teaspoon ground nutmeg	¼	cup cream

Melt 2 tablespoons of the butter and combine with 2 tablespoons of the sherry. Mop the shad inside and out with the butter-sherry mixture. Combine the next four seasoning ingredients. Use half of this mixture to season the shad. Refrigerate the seasoned shad and continue with the recipe, or refrigerate overnight.

Preheat oven to 400 degrees F. In a large, heavy saucepan over medium heat, fry the bacon until crisp and remove from the pan. Add the remaining butter and melt. Sauté the onions and celery. When the celery and onions are soft, add the shrimp and cook until opaque and the tails just begin to curl. Add the crab and bread crumbs. Blend together, then remove the pan from the heat. Combine the eggs, reserved seasoning, sherry, and half of the cream. Blend well and stuff the shad cavity with the mixture. Pour the remaining cream over the shad and bake for 1¼ hours (approximately 12 minutes per pound, with extra time for the stuffing).

4 servings

CREAMED ROE TOPPING

1	large shad roe		1	bay leaf
	Water		½	cup finely chopped onion
1	tablespoon vinegar			Salt and black pepper
½	teaspoon salt			

Cover the roe with water by 1 inch; add the vinegar, salt, bay leaf, and onion. Cook over low heat for 10 minutes or until the roe is firm. Remove the roe from the water, discarding the water, bay leaf, and onions. Remove the membranes from the roe and gently separate the eggs with a fork. Lightly salt and pepper the roe mixture. Gently spread over the fish just prior to adding the topping (below) and serving.

TOPPING

1	cup well-chilled heavy cream		2	tablespoons chopped fresh chives
4	teaspoons bottled horseradish			

In a chilled mixing bowl, beat the cream until it holds a soft peak. Add the horseradish and salt to taste. Spoon or pipe three dollops of cream on top of the fish, garnish with chives, and serve immediately.

Promises Made, Promises Kept

"[While at Hampton] I resolved that when I had finished the course of training I would go into the far South, into the Black Belt of the South, and give my life to providing the same kind of opportunity for self-reliance and self-awakening that I had found provided for me at Hampton. . . . with seventy-nine instructors, fourteen hundred acres of land, and thirty buildings, including large and small; in all, property valued at $280,000. Twenty-five industries have been organized [at Tuskegee]. . . ."

—Booker T. Washington, *The Awakening of the American Negro*, Atlantic Monthly 78, 1896

One-hundred-and-five years after publication of this article, Tuskegee University remains, "a strong and viable, institution, whose programs and services are known and respected throughout this country and in overseas places as well."

—Dr. Luther H. Foster, fourth president of Tuskegee University

Hampton and its progeny stand as a testament to the determination and perseverance of a generation of students who walked hundreds of miles toward the new freedom Hampton now represented. Students who, like Washington, spent a winter in the tents; suffered greatly and, bit by bit, helped build the legacy.

Hampton Teachers Answer
the Call to Service

Beloved teachers and friends returned and beloved teachers departed as they were called to service in the Hampton tradition. And Alice M. Bacon the "Little Professor" returned to Hampton. After visiting the neighborhood around the school, she became increasingly concerned with the health issues of ex-slaves. Finally after one of her students was repeatedly denied admittance to nursing schools, Alice Bacon proposed the establishment of a nursing school for the training of black practical nurses in the Hampton area. The school, which was to also have its own hospital to provide practical experience to the nurses, received strong support from General Armstrong.

Alice Bacon raised the $163,000.00 required to open the first formal training school for nurses in the south. And in May of 1982 the ten-bed, two-ward hospital, which opened in a building on Hampton's grounds, was christened "Dixie" after the horse Alice rode while visiting the sick. In attendance were one resident doctor and a superintendent of nurses.

On March 4, 1892, the Virginia General Assembly granted the Nurse's school the formal title of Hampton Training School for Nurses. Eventually as Hampton developed its own nursing program, Dixie was moved to the City of Hampton where it became known as Hampton General Hospital. And in Alice's final illness, it was one of Alice's "Dixie" nurses who cared for her.

Other beloved teachers were preparing to leave the school. ". . . Now after a stay of ten years as a resident graduate, I have been asked by two of the Hampton teachers to go with them to the black belt of Alabama and assist in lifting the cloud of ignorance . . . from my brothers and sisters. . . ."

—Georgia Washington, Hampton, Class of 1882

Georgia Washington Goes to Mt. Meigs, Alabama

Hampton graduates began returning to their homes to open schools, moving Booker T. Washington to comment that, "[The] Armstrong fire is spreading through the south." ". . . Women's hands light and dark had lighted that fire—still burning brightly—at Calhoun, Alabama, near its greater beacon at Tuskegee. For a year Georgia Washington helped Mabel Dillingham and Charlotte Thorne to kindle it there. . . ."

—Helen W. Ludlow, Hampton teacher

". . . The impulse to carry the torch farther came to [Georgia Washington] also . . . and with Godspeed from Calhoun and from Hampton, she bore the torch to a still darker center of the black belt, selected for her by Mr. Washington (no relation) near the small village of Mt. Meigs. . . ."

—Helen W. Ludlow

When Georgia Washington first arrived at Mt. Meigs, she found no building, no suitable place for a teacher to stay and parents too busy working cotton fields to meet with her. When asked what amount of property she owned, she replied, "my hands, head and heart." Clearly she had been educated for life; and her "capital" was about to pay big dividends.

After ten years, Georgia's guidance culminated in a community based project called the People's Village. ". . . Our enrollment for the first year had been one hundred children, . . . My only wish was for more than one tongue and one pair of hands and feet. I long for one of the trained girls from Hampton to join me in the work. . . ."

—Georgia Washington, Hampton Class of 1882

Not only one, but, three Hampton girls answered Georgia Washington's call for teachers and community women helped as well. ". . . Some of the [village] women rented a few acres and raised cotton to help with the work. Also, during cotton season, they charged each worker a one dollar tax as well. "Help also came from the north to those thus helping themselves."

—Georgia Washington, Hampton, Class of 1882

"... The Indian girls never forget to send a box ... to Alabama for the school founded by Miss Georgia Washington, ... who was once a beloved industrial teacher in the Winona family. ..."

—Helen W. Ludlow, Hampton teacher

Within ten years, "the old plantation on which cotton was being picked when Miss Washington arrived had become the property of the people and formed the school grounds and yard." As a result of Georgia Washington's example, "a new church had been built by the people; and a large two-story school building, accommodating three hundred is the crowning glory of the [Mt. Meig's People's Village School]. . . . The aim of the People's Village School is to prepare young men and women in simple, practical ways to go back to their homes and communities and give them a start. . . . At the People's Village School, "our studies are elementary. Bright and capable students we try to push toward . . . Hampton . . . to have them fitted to be teachers and leaders of our people along all lines. . . ."

—Georgia Washington

The bright and promising students were pushed toward Hampton in the same manner as Mr. Joseph Towe "a splendid teacher," pushed Georgia Washington, a former slave and the daughter of slaves.

In addition to building the school, Georgia Washington was instrumental in the organization of a savings and loan, which helped sharecroppers to buy their own land and build homes. She also organized mother's groups, which improved the quality of life in the community.

Samuel C. Armstrong had a vision, which he passed to his students. They in turn passed it to others and lives were changed. . . . Armstrong's vision caught like wildfire. . . . And the torch it lit was passed by light and brown hands. But the first sparks were lit at Hampton.

BAKED SHAD STUFFED WITH CORN BREAD

Two Virginia favorites, shad and corn bread, combine to bring one uniquely delicious dish to the dinner table.

1 5-pound shad, boned, split for stuffing, head and tail intact	1 large yellow onion, chopped
5 tablespoons bacon drippings, divided	1 cup chopped celery
Salt and black pepper to taste	1 cup chicken broth
1 teaspoon paprika	1 teaspoon garlic powder
1 large green bell pepper, seeded and chopped	½ teaspoon seasoned salt
	1½ cups crumbled corn bread
	Sliced onion

Preheat the oven to 400 degrees F. Prepare the fish and make three shallow slashes across its top side. Rub the fish inside and out with 1 tablespoon of the bacon drippings. Combine the salt, pepper, and paprika; mix well, and season the fish inside and out with the mixture. Refrigerate.

Sauté the green pepper, onion, and celery in the remaining bacon drippings until limp. Add the broth and bring to a boil. In a medium bowl, combine the sautéed vegetables, broth, garlic powder, seasoned salt, and crumbled corn bread; mix well. Place shad in a shallow baking pan, stuffing the cavity full and to just beyond the edge of the fish. Top with the sliced onion and bake for 45 minutes.

4 servings

SPICY BAKED SNAPPER

Snappers belong to a family of over seven hundred species of warm-water fish. They are mild and sweet, with a moist, moderately delicate texture and excellent flake. Select fish that are uniform in color, moist, and firm, with a fresh and mild aroma.

1	4- to 5-pound red snapper, cleaned, with head and tail intact	¾	teaspoon onion powder
3	garlic cloves, mashed	½	teaspoon lemon pepper
¼	cup vegetable oil	⅓	teaspoon garlic powder
½	cup fresh lime juice	¼	teaspoon ground allspice
1½	teaspoons seasoned salt	1¼	teaspoons paprika
		½	teaspoon cayenne pepper

Wash the snapper under running water and pat dry. Make three or four diagonal slices along each side of the fish. Place the snapper in a large, shallow baking dish. Combine garlic, vegetable oil, and lime juice. Pour this mixture inside and over snapper. Then combine the next seven seasoning ingredients and, reserving ¾ teaspoon of the spice mixture for later use, season the fish to taste by liberally rubbing the spice mixture into it, inside and out. Cover the fish and refrigerate for 2 hours, turning once during the marinating process. Meanwhile make the tomato sauce.

TOMATO SAUCE

¼	cup chopped green bell pepper	2	28-ounce cans Italian plum tomatoes, chopped; reserve 2 tomatoes, peeled, seeded, and chopped
1½	cups chopped yellow onion		
1	tablespoon minced garlic		
3	bay leaves	3	tablespoons tomato paste

In a large, heavy saucepan, sauté the pepper, onion, garlic, bay leaves, and ½ teaspoon of the remaining seasoning mix. When the onion is very soft and golden, stir in the tomatoes and juice, tomato paste, and ⅓ cup of the fish marinade. Bring the mixture to a quick boil, reduce the heat to medium low, and simmer for 30 to 45 minutes, or until very thick. Discard the bay leaves. Season to taste with the remaining seasoning mix.

Preheat the oven to 350 degrees F. Transfer the snapper with a spatula to a lightly oiled baking dish. Spoon approximately 1½ cups sauce inside the cavity. Pour half of the remaining sauce over the fish. Keep the remaining sauce covered and warm. Bake the snapper in the middle of the oven for 50 to 60 minutes or until it flakes. Using two spatulas, carefully transfer the fish to a large platter. Combine any pan drippings with the remaining sauce, mix well, and spoon over the snapper.

4 servings

BROILED LEMON PEPPER CATFISH

1	quart warm water	1	cup (2 sticks) butter, melted
2	teaspoons salt		Juice and zest of 1 lemon
4	whole catfish (approximately ½ to 1 pound each), cleaned, with heads removed	½	teaspoon seasoned salt
		½	teaspoon lemon pepper

Mix the water and salt, and soak the fish in this for 30 to 40 minutes. Drain well. Preheat the oven broiler. Combine the butter and the next three seasoning ingredients. Baste the fish on both sides with the butter mixture. Place in a shallow, greased boiler pan approximately 6 inches from the heat source. Cook for 5 to 7 minutes on each side, basting several times before turning. Cook until the fish is easily flaked with a fork but still moist. Be careful not to overcook.

4 servings

I says to my ol' ooman ez I watches down de lane,

"Don't you so't o' reckon, Lizy, dat we gwine to have some rain?"

"Go on, man," my Lizy answah, "you cain't fool me, not a bit,

I don't see no rain a-comin', ef you's wishin' fu it, quit;

Case de mo' you t'ink erbout it, an' de mo' you pray an' wish,

W'y de rain stay 'way de longah, spechul if you wants to fish."

But I see huh pat de skillet, an' I see huh cas' huh eye

Wid a kin o' anxious motion to'ds de da'kness in de sky;

An' I knows whut she's a-t'inkin, dough she tries so ha'd to hide.

She's a-sayin', "Wouldn't catfish now tas'e monst'ous bully, fried?"

—Excerpted from "Fishin'" by Paul Laurence Dunbar

FRIED CATFISH FILLETS

8–10	catfish fillets		¾	teaspoon sugar
	Salt and black pepper to taste		1	tablespoon flour
1	teaspoon seasoned salt		1¼	cups cornmeal
½	teaspoon ground black pepper		3	well-beaten eggs
¼	teaspoon paprika		¼	tablespoon bacon drippings
				Shortening sufficient for deep-frying

Wash the fish and pat dry. Lightly season with salt and pepper, then set aside. Combine the remaining six dry ingredients, mix well, and set aside. Dip the fillets first in the eggs, then in cornmeal mixture. Place on a waxed-paper-coated plate and refrigerate for at least 1 hour to allow the cornmeal coating to set. In a large, heavy skillet (preferably cast iron), heat the bacon drippings and shortening to 370 degrees F. The oil is sufficiently hot when a drop dances across its surface. Deep-fry the fish until golden brown.

Remove the fish to a paper-towel-lined plate to absorb the oil and serve immediately. When done, the fish should be opaque throughout and flake easily with a fork. Excellent with Coleslaw (see page 70) and Hush Puppies (page 183).

4 to 5 servings

Catfish fry
(Private collection, Carolyn Quick Tillery)

After a short walk across the Booker T. Washington Bridge, you'll come to a bridge walkway that takes you to the Hampton campus. Here on warm summer days you'll find the locals, casting an anxious eye to their line while hoping to reel in a fresh catch for dinner. . . .

PAN-FRIED VIRGINIA SPOTS

4	1-pound Virginia spots, cleaned, with heads intact	½	teaspoon black pepper
	Salt and black pepper to taste	¼	teaspoon paprika
1	cup cornmeal	⅛	teaspoon cayenne pepper
½	cup all-purpose flour	¼	cup (½ stick) butter
1	teaspoon salt	½	cup solid shortening

Wash the fish and pat dry. (Leave the heads intact to preserve the piece of "sweet meat" found on top of the head.) Season the fish to taste, inside and out, with salt and pepper, then set aside. Combine the remaining six dry ingredients and mix well. Dredge the fish in this mixture, coating well, and shake off any excess. In a heavy 12-inch skillet (preferably cast iron), heat the butter and shortening to 370 degrees F. The oil is sufficiently hot when a drop of water dances across its surface. Fry the fish for about 8 to 10 minutes on each side until golden. The fish is done when the flesh is opaque and flakes easily with a fork. Remove the fish to a paper-towel-lined plate to absorb the oil, and serve immediately.

4 servings

PAN FRIED CROAKERS

4 1-pound croakers, cleaned and scored, heads intact	½ teaspoon powdered ginger
1 cup clam juice	⅛ teaspoon ground allspice
2 tablespoons lime juice	½ teaspoon salt
2 tablespoons lemon juice	¼ teaspoon cayenne pepper
⅛ teaspoon Liquid Smoke	¼ teaspoon ground black pepper
¼ teaspoon ground nutmeg	1 tablespoon grated lemon peel
⅛ teaspoon Tabasco sauce	2 tablespoons grated onion
	1 garlic clove, crushed

Mix together all of the ingredients (except the fish). Pour the marinade over the scored fish, and refrigerate. Allow to marinate for a minimum of 2 hours, or overnight. Turn several times during the process. Take care not to marinate unevenly or more than the recommended time or the fish will become too acidic.

FISH COATING

1 cup yellow cornmeal	½ teaspoon ground black pepper
¼ cup flour	¼ teaspoon dry mustard
1½ teaspoons paprika	½ teaspoon onion powder
½ teaspoon cayenne pepper	¼ teaspoon garlic powder
1 teaspoon seasoned salt	

Combine the above ingredients (except the cayenne pepper) and set aside. Remove the fish from the marinade and dredge in seasoned cornmeal; shake off the excess. In a large cast-iron skillet, heat drippings or shortening to a depth of ½ inch over medium heat to 370 degrees F. The oil is sufficiently hot when a drop of water dances across its surface. Fry the fish for about 5 to 10 minutes on each side. The frying time will vary according to the size and thickness of the fish. Fry until the fish is crispy brown and its flesh flakes easily and appears opaque. Remove the fish to a paper-towel-lined plate to absorb the oil.

Next, remove all but ¼ cup of the drippings from the pan and add the reserved marinade and cayenne pepper. Bring to a quick boil; boil for an additional 5 minutes and use as an optional seasoning garnish.

4 servings

SHRIMP WITH RICE

5	large tomatoes
8	bacon slices, diced into ¼-inch cubes
2	cups chopped yellow onions
½	cup chopped green bell pepper
3	garlic cloves, minced
2	cups raw rice
2	teaspoons seasoned salt
¾	teaspoon cayenne pepper
¼	teaspoon ground cumin
2½	teaspoons Worcestershire sauce
2	tablespoons finely chopped parsley
3	cups hot chicken broth
2½	pounds large raw shrimp, shelled and deveined

Cut the tomatoes in half, crosswise. Gently squeeze the tomatoes to remove the seeds and juice, then coarsely chop. In a large skillet, fry the bacon over medium-high heat. When the bacon is crisp, remove it from the pan to a paper-towel-lined plate and set aside. Add the onions, green pepper, garlic, rice, salt, cayenne pepper, and cumin. Continue to cook over medium-high heat, stirring, until the rice is golden. Add the Worcestershire, parsley, and chicken broth. Bring to a boil, reduce the heat to medium, cover, and cook for 10 minutes. Add the shrimp, cover, and cook for 10 additional minutes or until the shrimp are pink, opaque, and tender, and all the liquid has been absorbed. Remove to a serving dish. Crumble the reserved bacon over the shrimp and rice before serving.

4 servings

FRIED CRAB PATTIES

2	tablespoons butter
2½	tablespoons finely chopped onion
2½	tablespoons minced green bell pepper
1½	tablespoons minced celery
1	pound fresh lump crabmeat, well drained
1	cup prepared mashed potatoes
1	large egg, beaten
1	teaspoon Worcestershire sauce
1	tablespoon whipping cream
¼	teaspoon garlic powder
½	teaspoon onion powder
	Salt and black pepper to taste
	Flour
⅓	cup shortening plus 2 tablespoons butter, for frying

In a large skillet, melt the 2 tablespoons of butter and sauté the onion, green pepper, and celery over medium heat. Cook until the onion is soft and transparent, and set aside. In a separate bowl, combine the remaining ingredients (except the flour, shortening, and butter). Add the vegetable mixture to the bowl and mix lightly. Shape into four flat cakes, and dust lightly with flour. Heat the shortening and butter in a large skillet over medium-high heat. Place the crab cakes in the skillet and fry until golden, 3 to 4 minutes on each side. When done, remove to a paper-towel-lined plate to drain. Serve immediately with Tartar Sauce (page 132).

4 servings

FRIED SOFT-SHELL CRABS

1	dozen soft-shell crabs, cleaned		1	teaspoon seasoned salt
4	eggs		1¼	teaspoons ground white pepper
1	cup flour		⅛	teaspoon cayenne pepper
				Vegetable oil for frying

Wash the crabs under cold running water and pat dry with paper towels. Lightly beat the eggs and set aside. Combine the flour and remaining ingredients. Lightly dust the crabs with the flour mixture. Dip in beaten eggs and flour again. In a heavy cast-iron skillet, heat ½ inch of vegetable oil to 350 degrees F. (If the oil is not sufficiently hot, the crabs will be greasy.) Place the crabs back side down in the hot oil and brown well. Turn and brown other side. Remove to a paper towel to drain. Serve with Tartar Sauce (page 132).

4 servings

SOFT-SHELL CRAB SANDWICHES

4   soft-shell crabs, cleaned
¾   cup melted butter
¾   cup green onions, chopped,
       including tops
3   large garlic cloves, minced fine
1   teaspoon Old Bay Seafood
       Seasoning (page 110)

2   teaspoons Worcestershire sauce
¼   teaspoon Tabasco sauce
⅛   teaspoon dry mustard
⅛   teaspoon paprika
⅛   teaspoon cayenne pepper
     Thick Italian sourdough bread
2   tablespoons sour cream

Preheat the oven to 350 degrees F. Wash the crabs under cold running water and pat dry with paper towels. Combine the melted butter, green onions, garlic, Old Bay Seafood Seasoning, Worcestershire, Tabasco, and spices. Season the crabs to taste with additional Old Bay Seafood Seasoning. Place half of the butter mixture on the bottom of an 8- to 12-inch pan. Spread the remaining sauce on top of the crabs. Bake for 20 to 30 minutes until golden brown and baked through. Place each crab on a slice of bread. Blend the sour cream into the pan drippings. Spoon the sauce over each crab and top with another slice of bread.

4 servings

SAVORY SALMON CROQUETTES

3   tablespoons butter, melted
¼   cup flour
1   cup heavy cream
1   teaspoon salt
1   teaspoon ground black
       pepper
     1-pound cold salmon,
       skinned, deboned, and
       cooked (*or* 1 16-ounce can)
¼   cup (½ stick) butter

1   medium yellow onion, chopped fine
1   small green bell pepper, chopped
       fine
½   cup soft bread crumbs
1   egg
     Flour
¼   cup vegetable oil, for frying
     Parsley sprigs and lemon wedges,
       for garnish

In a bowl, blend together the melted butter and flour and set aside. In a medium saucepan, bring the cream to a slow boil. Add the butter-flour mixture and rapidly whisk until blended smooth. Whisk while cooking for an additional 10 minutes. Remove from the heat and add the salt, pepper, and salmon. Mix thoroughly and then turn out onto a dish to cool. While the mixture is cooling, heat a large, heavy skillet over medium heat; add the ¼ cup of butter and sauté the onion and green pepper until the onion is transparent. Add the contents of the frying pan and the bread crumbs to the cooled salmon mixture. If the mixture appears too dry, add additional cream. If it appears too soft, add additional bread crumbs. Form six patties; dust the patties with flour, roll them in beaten eggs, and then dust with flour again. Cook the cakes in vegetable oil over medium heat until cooked through and golden, about 5 minutes on each side. Garnish with parsley and lemon.

Yields 4 to 6 patties

MOM'S DEVILISH CATFISH STEW

This recipe takes its name from the fact that it is unusually hot. Novices, however, may reduce the amount of pepper called for in this recipe and still enjoy the unusual flavor of this tasty dish, which actually is a version of smothered catfish.

6–8	catfish fillets		¼	cup oil
	Salt and black pepper to taste		1	onion, sliced thin
½–1	teaspoon cayenne pepper, to taste		2	jalapeño peppers, seeded and chopped
	Flour			

Wash the fillets and season to taste. Dust with flour, shaking off any excess. Heat the oil in a large, heavy skillet over medium heat. The oil is sufficiently hot when a drop of water dances on the surface. Add the fillets to the pan, turning frequently to prevent burning. When fillets are done (about 3 to 4 minutes total on each side), remove them to a paper-towel-covered plate and keep warm.

After all fillets have been cooked, add the onion and jalapeño to the pan and sauté until the onion is transparent. Place approximately ¼ cup of the remaining dusting flour in the pan. Cook until the flour browns, then add 2 cups of hot water. Reduce the heat and cook until the gravy begins to thicken. Season to taste with additional salt, pepper, and cayenne pepper. Return the fillets to the pan and cook for an additional 10 to 15 minutes over low heat. Serve with hot, fluffy white rice.

4 to 6 servings

CREAM OF CRABMEAT AND SHRIMP SOUP

½	cup minced onion	¼	teaspoon onion powder
3	tablespoons unsalted butter	¼	teaspoon seasoned salt
½	cup flour	½	teaspoon Tabasco sauce
¼	cup sherry	2	cups half-and-half
2	cups bottled clam juice	1	pound lump crabmeat, picked over
¼	teaspoon Old Bay Seafood Seasoning (page 110)	½	pound baby shrimp

In a large saucepan, sauté the onion in the butter over medium-low heat. Whisk in the flour and continue to whisk for 3 minutes. Next, whisk in the sherry, clam juice, Old Bay Seafood Seasoning, onion powder, seasoned salt, Tabasco sauce, and half-and-half. Simmer the mixture, whisking occasionally, for 15 minutes. Add the crabmeat and shrimp, and continue to cook until heated through.

4 servings

SOUTHERN CLAM CHOWDER

5	bacon slices, chopped	1	potato, peeled and cubed
2	medium onions, chopped	2	bay leaves
1	cup green bell pepper, chopped	½	cup minced onion
2	celery stalks, chopped fine	½	teaspoon seasoned salt
2	large garlic cloves, minced fine	¼	teaspoon dried basil
4	large tomatoes, chopped	3	10-ounce cans chopped clams, undrained
3	cups clam juice	½	pound boiled okra, sliced
		½	pound small bay scallops

In a large saucepan, sauté the bacon over medium heat until it's transparent. Add the onions, green pepper, celery, and garlic. Sauté until the onions are transparent. Add the tomatoes, clam juice, potato, bay leaves, and remaining three seasoning ingredients. Bring to a boil; reduce the heat, cover, and simmer until the potato is cooked through, 30 to 45 minutes. Stir in the clams, cooked okra, and bay scallops for the last 3 to 5 minutes of cooking. Take care not to overcook the bay scallops, or they will become rubbery. Remove bay leaves before serving.

4 servings

STOVETOP CLAM BAKE

4	kale leaves	8	half ears corn, fresh or frozen
½	cup clam juice	12	clams
¼	cup white wine	12	mussels
8	small red potatoes, unpeeled	12	oysters
8	small onions, peeled		Melted butter
1	lobster		Lemon wedges

Place the kale leaves, clam juice, and wine in the bottom of a large heavy pot. Lay the potatoes and onions on top. Cover tightly and steam for 15 minutes. Kill the lobster by severing the spinal cord with a large heavy knife inserted between the body and tail sections; cut it into eight pieces. Add the corn lobster, and clams to the pot and steam for 10 minutes. Add the mussels and the oysters. Steam until the clams and mussels open, approximately 10 minutes. Serve with melted butter and lemon wedges.

4 servings

SEAFOOD OKRA GUMBO

1½ cups bacon drippings, divided	2½ cups seeded and chopped fresh tomatoes
2 cups sliced okra	1 6-ounce can tomato paste
3 tablespoons flour	7 cups water
1 cup cold water	1½ pounds large shrimp, washed, peeled, and deveined
2 onions, chopped fine	24 oysters in their liquor
¼ cup chopped celery	½ teaspoon Tabasco sauce
1 green bell pepper, seeded and chopped	1 tablespoon Worcestershire sauce
3 medium jalapeño peppers, seeded and chopped	1 pound claw crabmeat
3 garlic cloves, peeled and minced	2 teaspoons salt
3 large bay leaves	½ teaspoon cayenne pepper

In a large, heavy skillet (not cast iron), heat ¼ cup of the bacon drippings. Add the okra and cook, stirring often, until stringing stops. Add additional bacon drippings (up to ¼ cup) as necessary to prevent burning. Place the cooked okra in a bowl and set aside. Wash the pan and return it to the stove. Add ½ cup of the remaining drippings and gradually stir in the flour. Stir constantly until a dark brown roux forms. Add 1 cup of cold water and stir, mixing well. Remove the pan from the heat and set aside.

In a large pot, heat the remaining ½ cup of drippings over medium-high heat until a haze begins to form above the skillet. Add the onions, celery, and peppers; sauté, stirring constantly, until the onions are transparent. Add the garlic and bay leaves; stir and reduce the heat to low. Stir in the tomatoes and tomato paste. Add as much of the 7 cups of water to the roux pan as necessary to deglaze it. Transfer the mixture and any remaining water to the vegetable mixture in the pot. Stir until smooth. Bring to a boil, reduce the heat, and add the okra. Cover and simmer over low heat for 1 hour. Add the shrimp and oysters with their liquor and cook for 10 minutes. If the gumbo is too thick, thin with water. Add remaining ingredients. Serve over a mound of steamed rice.

4 to 6 servings

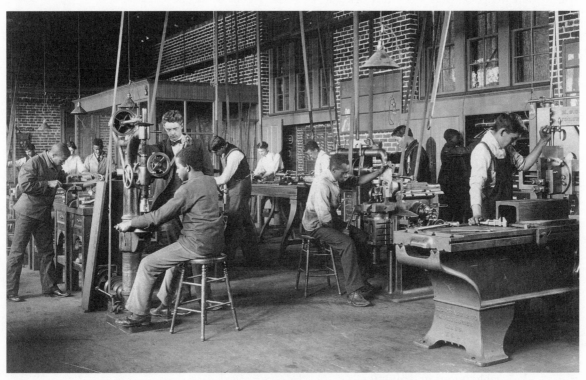

Young men training in use of machinery
(Reproduced from the collections of the Library of Congress)

PAN-FRIED OYSTERS

24	ounces fresh oysters, shucked		Pinch of cayenne pepper
2	eggs, well beaten	1½	cups bread crumbs
2	tablespoons half-and-half	1½	cups flour
¾	teaspoon salt	¾	teaspoon seasoned salt
⅛	teaspoon white pepper		Lemon wedges

Drain the oysters and set aside. Combine the eggs, half-and-half, and next three seasoning ingredients. In a separate container, combine bread crumbs, flour, and seasoned salt. Roll the oysters in the seasoned crumb mixture. Dip them in the egg mixture, and roll again in the crumb mixture. Dip in the egg and then the crumb mixture one additional time for a thicker coating. Fry in hot fat over moderate heat until brown on one side. Turn carefully and brown on the other side. Drain on absorbent paper towels. Serve with lemon wedges, Tartar Sauce (below), and Oyster Cocktail Sauce (also below).

4 servings

TARTAR SAUCE

2	cups mayonnaise	2½	tablespoons dill relish
¼	cup minced onion	2	tablespoons sweet relish
1½	teaspoons finely chopped parsley	1	tablespoon Worcestershire sauce
2	tablespoons capers, drained		

Combine all of the above ingredients and refrigerate for an hour or two before serving to develop the flavor.

Yields 2¼ cups

OYSTER COCKTAIL SAUCE

2	cups ketchup	1½	tablespoons minced celery
3½	tablespoons prepared horseradish	½	teaspoon salt
3½	tablespoons white vinegar	1¼	teaspoons Tabasco sauce
2½	tablespoons grated onion	1	teaspoon Worcestershire sauce

Mix the above ingredients and chill for 1 or 2 hours to develop the flavor. Serve with oysters.

Yields ½ cup

Class in capillary physics
(Reproduced from the collections of the Library of Congress)

A class in woodworking
(Reproduced from the collections of the Library of Congress)

BUFFALO CLAM STRIPS

Chef Adam Lindstrom, Radisson Hotel, Hampton

5   pounds large chowder clams,
      shucked and cut in strips
4   cups flour

1   cup Cajun seasoning
6   egg yolks, well beaten

Combine the flour and Cajun seasoning, mix well, and set aside. Prepare the clams and refrigerate until ready for use. Dip the clam strips in the flour mixture. Next, dip the strips in the egg yolks and then back in the flour mixture. Deep-fry until golden brown.

6 to 8 servings

Hampton students studying cannon at Fortress Monroe
(Reproduced from the collections of the Library of Congress)

Girls measuring a piece of land in arithmetic class
(Reproduced from the collections of the Library of Congress)

VEGETABLES

"Market-gardening is carried on extensively, hundreds of dollars' worth of aspara-gus, cabbages, white and sweet potatoes, . . . and peas being annually sold at Fortress Monroe or shipped to the markets of Baltimore, Philadelphia, New-York and Boston.

"The market wagon runs daily with milk and vegetables, and the meat wagon three times a week to Hampton and Old Point Comfort. Peaches, potatoes, and cabbages are shipped to Baltimore and the north with very satisfactory returns, and the board-ing department is principally supplied from the farm."

—Samuel C. Armstrong

GLAZED ACORN SQUASH

During a recent visit to my brother-in-law, Bill Tillery's home in Dallas, he served a similar squash dish with his Sunday Turkey and Dressing dinner. He boils his turkey before baking it. It's always delicious and we always request it. I am still working on enticing the turkey recipe from him for my next book.

6	small acorn squash		¼	cup honey
1	tablespoon lemon juice		⅓	cup unsalted butter
2	cups boiling apple juice		½	cup firmly packed brown sugar

Preheat the oven to 375 degrees F. Quarter the squash lengthwise. Scoop out the seeds and stringy fiber and discard. Pierce each squash piece with a fork several times. Place the squash pieces in a large baking dish. Combine the lemon juice, apple juice, honey, and butter; mix well. Pour this mixture over the squash, then cover the dish tightly with aluminum foil and bake until very tender, approximately 20 to 25 minutes. Transfer the squash to a large cookie sheet. Prepare the glaze (below) and brush over the squash. Bake the squash, uncovered, until deep golden brown, approximately 15 minutes. Baste occasionally with glaze. Transfer the squash to a platter or individual serving plates.

6 to 8 servings

GLAZE

6	tablespoons melted butter		Pinch of ground allspice
¼	cup dark brown sugar		Pinch of ground nutmeg
¼	teaspoon ground cinnamon		

Combine all of the above ingredients in a small bowl and use to baste squash quarters.

YELLOW SQUASH AND ONIONS

1   large onion, sliced thin
3   tablespoons bacon drippings
1   small garlic clove, minced
     fine
2   pounds yellow squash, sliced
     to a ¼-inch thickness

2   tablespoons water
     Salt and black pepper to taste
¼   cup chopped chives

In a large, covered skillet, sauté the onion over medium heat in the bacon drippings until soft and transparent. Add the garlic, squash, and water. Cover and reduce the heat to low. Cook to your desired tenderness, 15 to 20 minutes. Season with salt and pepper to taste. Add the chives, mix well, and cook for another 2 or 3 minutes.

TURNIP GREENS

Turnip greens are excellent alone in this recipe, but they can also be mixed with pokeweed or other wild greens.

2   smoked ham hocks or
     smoked turkey wings
4   cups water, or sufficient to
     cover meat
1   small onion, chopped
3   jalapeño peppers, chopped
1   tablespoon sugar

1   teaspoon crushed red pepper
2   pounds fresh turnip greens, cleaned
     and cut up
1½   teaspoons salt
1   teaspoon garlic powder
1   teaspoon ground black pepper
4   peeled, pared, and quartered turnips

Add the ham hocks or turkey wings to boiling water in a large pot. Reduce the heat, cover, and simmer for 1 hour. Add the next four ingredients, followed by the turnip greens. Reduce the heat to medium low, cover the pot tightly, and simmer for 1 hour. Check often and add water as necessary to prevent burning. Add the remaining ingredients and allow to simmer for an additional 30 to 45 minutes or until the greens are tender.

6 servings

Old-Fashioned Green Beans With Garden Potatoes

2 pounds green beans	1 tablespoon brown sugar
1 small onion, chopped	2 ham hocks *or* 1 ham bone
2 tablespoons bacon drippings	1 teaspoon seasoned salt
1 garlic clove, crushed	½ teaspoon onion powder
1 quart water	½ teaspoon garlic powder
⅛ teaspoon Liquid Smoke	4 large new potatoes, quartered

String the beans, wash, and set aside. In a large pot, sauté the onion over medium heat in the bacon drippings until transparent. Add the garlic and sauté for an additional minute. Add the water, Liquid Smoke, brown sugar, and ham hocks or ham bone. Bring to a rapid boil over high heat. Reduce the heat to low and simmer the ham hocks for 1½ hours, adding water as necessary to prevent sticking. Add the seasoned salt, onion powder, and garlic powder. Stir and add the green beans. Cover the pot and simmer over low heat until the beans are tender, approximately 30 to 40 minutes. Add the potatoes during the last 30 minutes of cooking and continue to cook until they're fork-tender.

6 servings

Green Beans and Corn

Old-fashioned beans were cooked for an extended period of time because they were tougher. Today's beans require less cooking time; you can adjust this time to your taste.

2	pounds green beans, ends and strings removed	1	teaspoon seasoned salt
1	ham hock	½	teaspoon onion powder
1	small onion, chopped	1	teaspoon brown sugar
2	tablespoons bacon drippings	2	ears corn, cut into thirds
1	quart water		Salt and black pepper to taste

Wash the green beans and ham hock separately; set both aside to drain. In a large pot, over medium heat, sauté the onion in the bacon drippings. Add the water, spices, sugar, and ham hock; bring to a rapid boil over high heat. Reduce the heat to low and simmer for 1 hour. Add the beans, cover, and cook for an additional 45 minutes. If needed, add additional water sufficient to cook without burning. Add the corn and continue to cook for half an hour. Add salt and pepper to taste.

6 servings

Corn on the Cob

There's nothing quite like biting into the crunchy goodness of sweet corn. The old-fashioned standard sweet corns, such as Silver Queen, Golden Bantam, and the like, lose their sweetness and become starchy within a couple of hours of picking, especially when left unrefrigerated. Adding sugar to the cooking water helps restore some of this sweetness. The newer supersweet, extra-sweet, and sugar-enhanced varieties remain sweet and crisp for many hours after being picked. When buying corn, look for young, tender kernels that have a milky inside when split open. Depending on appetite, most people eat from two to four ears at one sitting.

4	quarts water	Butter
2	teaspoons sugar	Salt and black pepper to taste
8	ears of corn	

Bring the water to a boil and add the sugar (do not add the salt yet, as it tends to toughen the corn). Place the corn, four ears at a time, in the boiling water, bring to a second boil, and cook for 2 additional minutes. The older the corn, the longer the required cooking time. Remove with tongs, and cook the second batch while eating the first. Place the cooked corn in a cotton-napkin-lined dish. Cover the corn with an additional napkin so that it retains its heat. Serve with butter, salt, and pepper. There is nothing so satisfying or delicious as biting into an ear of corn with kernels so crunchy and tender that they spurt sweet juice.

4 to 6 servings

The Decision to Begin a Great Work

"I wish to make my institution excel in whatever it undertakes."
—General Samuel C. Armstrong, August 1868

Yet when General Armstrong started all he had was a vision, his hands, his head; and most important his heart.

". . . On my first visit to Hampton I met General Armstrong in the library. He took me to the window and said . . . He should never forget the hour spent with Mr. Smith . . . it was before the land had been purchased for school purposes. The General and Mr. Smith saw that the situation was admirable for the work the General was planning. . . . The land was at that date offered for sale and $9,000.00 must be paid down or the land could not be kept for the General's work.

   " 'Shall we take the land to build a school. . . . Shall we take it,' they asked each other again and again. Then they walked silently for many minutes when Mr. Smith broke the silence by saying, 'General, take the land.' The General said, 'Where's the money?' . . . 'Take the land,' said Mr. Smith, 'the money will come.' Before the day for payment arrived a legacy of $10,000.00 [that] was left to be invested in [the] work."

—from *Memories of Old Hampton*

STEAMED CORN

½   cup water
½   teaspoon sugar

8   ears of corn

Place the water and sugar in a large pot, add four ears of corn, and cover the pot. Bring the water to a boil. Cook for 5 minutes. Uncover and serve immediately. To increase servings, halve the ears. Repeat the process to cook the remaining corn.

4 to 8 servings

ROASTED FRESH CORN ON THE COB

8   ears of fresh, tender roasting
     corn

Water to cover
1½   teaspoons sugar

Pull down the corn husks to remove the corn silk. Soak the corn in sugared water for 10 minutes. Replace the husks and close with a twisting motion or tie closed. Arrange the ears around the outer edges of a grill about 4 inches above hot coals. Roast for 15 to 20 minutes, turning the ears every 3 to 4 minutes. They can also be roasted in the oven at 400 degrees F. for 15 minutes. Remove the husks. Serve with butter, salt, and pepper.

6 to 8 servings

MINTED CARROTS

3 pounds carrots, peeled and cut diagonally into ¼-inch-thick slices	3 tablespoons sugar
1 tablespoon lime juice	1 teaspoon salt
3 cups water	3 tablespoons butter
	2 tablespoons coarsely cut fresh mint leaves

In a large, heavy saucepan, combine the carrots and the next four ingredients, bring to a boil, reduce the heat, cover, and simmer until the carrots are tender, approximately 15 to 20 minutes. Drain the carrots and stir in the butter. Adjust the seasonings to taste and toss lightly with the mint.

6 to 8 servings

HONEY-GLAZED CARROTS

3 pounds carrots, peeled and cut diagonally into ¼-inch-thick slices	3 tablespoons butter
1½ cups orange juice	2 tablespoons brown sugar
1½ cups water	3 tablespoons honey
1 teaspoon salt	⅛ teaspoon ground nutmeg
	1 teaspoon grated orange rind

In a large, heavy saucepan, combine the carrots and the next three ingredients, bring to a boil, reduce the heat, cover, and simmer until the carrots are tender, approximately 15 to 20 minutes. Drain the carrots and set aside.

In a large, heavy skillet, over medium-high heat, melt the butter, add the sugar, and stir until it dissolves. Add the remaining ingredients. Mix well and add the carrots, coating them with the glaze. Cover and allow to stand for 20 minutes. Rewarm just prior to serving.

6 to 8 servings

Creamed Peas and Pearl Onions

30	small peeled white onions (approximately 1 inch in diameter)	2	teaspoons sugar
¼	teaspoon salt	5	tablespoons butter
2	pounds fresh green peas (frozen may be substituted)	3	tablespoons cornstarch
		2	cups light cream
		¼–½	teaspoon ground nutmeg

Place the onions in a medium pot with enough water to cover them by 1 inch. Add the salt and bring to a boil. Reduce the heat to low and simmer, partially covered, for approximately 20 minutes. Reserving the cooking water for later use, drain the onions and set aside. Next, cook the fresh peas by placing them in 6 to 7 quarts of rapidly boiling water. Stir in the sugar and allow peas to cook for 8 to 10 minutes or until tender. Quickly drain the peas and immediately immerse them in cold water to stop the cooking process and preserve the bright green color. In a heavy saucepan, melt the butter over moderate heat and stir in the cornstarch. Remove the pan from the heat and stir in 2 cups of reserved onion water. Beat the mixture for 2 or 3 minutes until almost smooth, add the cream, return the pan to a moderate burner, and heat, while constantly whisking, until the sauce is thick and smooth. Simmer for 3 minutes. Add the peas and onions, and simmer for 5 additional minutes or until the peas and onions are heated through. Stir in nutmeg and serve immediately.

4 to 6 servings

Baked Onion Casserole

18	whole small white onions, up to an inch in diameter		Pinch of ground nutmeg
2	tablespoons butter	1	cup evaporated milk
2	tablespoons all-purpose flour	1	small bay leaf
¼	teaspoon salt	½	cup buttered bread crumbs
			Paprika

Preheat the oven to 400 degrees F. Butter a 1-quart casserole dish and set aside. Boil the onions in salted water until tender; drain and set aside. In a saucepan, over medium heat, melt the butter and stir in the flour, salt, and nutmeg. Add the milk and continue to cook over medium heat, stirring constantly, until smooth. Add the bay leaf and continue to cook for an additional 5 minutes or until the mixture begins to thicken. Remove the bay leaf. Place the onions in the prepared casserole and pour the sauce over them. Top with buttered bread crumbs, sprinkle with paprika, and bake for 15 minutes or until brown and bubbly.

6 to 8 servings

SWEET TURNIPS AND CARROTS

½ teaspoon salt	2 tablespoons sugar
1 large yellow turnip, peeled and quartered	2 tablespoons butter
6 large carrots, peeled and sliced ¼ inch thick	¼ cup heavy cream
	¼ teaspoon freshly grated nutmeg

Place the salt, turnip, and carrots in a medium saucepan, add sufficient water to cover the vegetables by 2 inches, and bring to a boil. Add additional water as necessary to permit the vegetables to freely boil and prevent sticking. When the vegetables are soft enough to mash, drain away the water and add the sugar, butter, cream, and nutmeg. Mash with a potato masher and stir until smooth and well blended.

4 to 6 servings

OKRA WITH CORN AND TOMATOES

3	cups very cold water	2	cups corn cut from the cob
1	tablespoon fresh lemon juice	1	cup fresh tomato, peeled, seeded and chopped
1½	cups sliced okra		Salt and freshly ground black pepper to taste
½	cup minced onion		
½	teaspoon minced garlic		
2	tablespoons bacon drippings		

Combine the water and lemon juice and soak the okra in this mixture for 30 minutes to help remove gumminess. Remove the okra to a colander and drain well. In a large cast-iron skillet, sauté the onion and garlic in the bacon drippings over medium heat. Add the okra and continue to sauté over medium heat for approximately 5 minutes, stirring constantly. Reduce the heat, add the remaining ingredients, and simmer for approximately 20 minutes. Add water as necessary to prevent sticking.

4 to 6 servings

FRIED TOMATOES WITH BROWN SAUCE

2½	teaspoons salt	3	eggs
1	teaspoon white pepper	2	teaspoons water
¼	teaspoon cayenne pepper	6	ripe tomatoes, sliced
⅛	teaspoon ground nutmeg	2	cups fine dry bread crumbs

Combine the salt and the next three seasoning ingredients; mix well and set aside. Combine the eggs and water; mix well and set aside. Next, having selected firm but ripe tomatoes of uniform size, wash them thoroughly and cut into ½-inch slices. Use the salt mixture to season the tomatoes to taste. Dip the tomato slices in the bread crumbs, then in the eggs, and back in the bread crumbs again. Place on a wire rack and allow to dry for 10 minutes.

In a large cast-iron skillet, fry the tomatoes in ½ inch of hot shortening over medium-high heat. Fry in a single layer, without crowding the pan. The tomatoes are done when they are brown on each side and tender. Serve immediately with Brown Sauce (recipe follows).

4 to 6 servings

An American Indian in American history class
(Courtesy of Hampton University Archives)

BROWN SAUCE

2½ tablespoons bacon drippings	¼ teaspoon black pepper
2 tablespoons flour	1 cup hot beef stock
¼ teaspoon salt	¼ teaspoon Worcestershire sauce

Melt the drippings over medium-high heat. Add the flour, salt, and pepper, and brown to a rich reddish brown color, without burning. Slowly stir in the hot beef broth. Continue stirring as the broth thickens to a satisfactory consistency. Then remove the sauce from the heat, add the Worcestershire, mix well, and serve hot over fried tomatoes.

A Letter

Paul Laurence Dunbar

. . . I'se feeling kin'o' homesick—dat's ez nachul ez cin be,

W'en a feller's mo'n th'ee thousand miles across dat awful sea.

(don't you let nobidy fool you 'bout de ocean bein' gran';

If you want to see de billers, you jes' view em f'om de lan'.)

'Bout de people? We been t'inkin' dat all white folks was alak;

But dese Englishmen is diffunt, an' dey's curus fu' a fac'.

Fust, dey's heavier an' redder in dey make-up an' dey looks

An dey don't put salt nor pepper in a blessed t'ing dey cooks!

W'en dey gin you good ol' tu'nips, ca'ots, pa' snips, beets, an' sich,

Ef dey ain't some one to tell you, you cain't stinuish which is which.

W'en I t'ought I's eatin' chicken—you may b'liev dis hyeah's a lie—

But de waiter beat me down dat I was eatin' rabbit pie. . . .

O, hit's mighty nice, dis trav'lin, an' I's kin' o' glad I come.

But, I reckon, now I's willin fu' to tek my way back home. . . .

Dough my appetite 'ud call me, ef dey wasn't nuffin else.

I'd jes' lak to have some sweet-pertaters roasted in de skin;

I's a-longin' fu' my chittlin's an' my mustard greens ergin;

I's a-wishin' fu some buttermilk, an' co'n braid, good an' brown,

An' a drap o' good ol' bourbon fu' to wash my feelin's down! . . .

Tell de folks I sen' 'em howdy; gin a kiss to pap an' mam;

Closin' I is, deah Miss Lucy,

Still Yo' Own True-Lovin Sam.

PICKLED BEETS AND ONIONS

1	12-ounce can sliced beets, juice reserved	5	whole cloves
2	tablespoons oil	1	teaspoon sugar
1	tablespoon vinegar	½	teaspoon salt
		1	onion, sliced thin

Drain the beet juice into a serving dish. Blend in the oil, vinegar, cloves, sugar, and salt. Add the beets and onion; refrigerate for at least 1 hour before serving.

4 to 6 servings

An American Indian student at Hampton
(Courtesy of Hampton University Archives)

CABBAGE

3	hickory-smoked bacon slices	¼	cup water
1	medium onion, peeled and sliced thin		Salt and black pepper to taste
1	medium cabbage, sliced	3	tablespoons heavy cream

In a medium saucepan over medium heat, sauté the bacon until transparent. Add the sliced onion and stir constantly for 2 minutes, or until the onion is transparent. Add the cabbage and water. Reduce the heat to low, cover, and simmer undisturbed for 10 minutes. Remove the lid and stir. Cover the pot again and simmer for an additional 10 or 15 minutes or until the cabbage is tender. Salt and pepper to taste. Stir in the cream and allow to stand for a few minutes to permit the cabbage to absorb the seasoning.

4 to 6 servings

. . . When de cabbage pot is steamin'

An' de bacon good an' fat,

When de chittlins is a-sputter'n'

So's to show you whah dey's at;

Tek away yo' sody biscuit,

Tek away yo' cake an' pie,

Fu' de glory time is comin',

An' its 'proachin' mighty nigh,

An' you want to jump an' hollah,

Dough you know you'd bettah not,

When yo' mammy days de blessin'

An' de co'n pone's hot.

—Excerpted from "When De Co'n Pone's Hot"
by Paul Laurence Dunbar

The Making of a Future College President

"That night I took the same steamer on which I had arrived and landed at Old Point the following morning, the 13th of October, 1885. I took a hack, which carried me and my little trunk past Fortress Monroe and up through the little town of Phoebus, then Mill Creek, and on to the grounds of the Hampton Institute. It was to me the most beautiful place I had ever seen. . . . We drove up through the school farm past the old Butler School. This was a school that had been built under the direction of General Butler during the Civil War for the children of the freedmen, out of the lumber that had been used, much of it, in hospital barracks. . . . We passed on through many acres of vegetables which Hampton had cultivated. . . . Looking upon the well kept grounds of the Institute, the water front, the neat and imposing buildings and farm lands, I felt almost as if I were in another world. . . .

"[Finally] . . . I presented myself to the commandant, the Rev. George L. Curtis [who] sent me for examination to Miss Anna G. Baldwin, the head teacher in the night school. . . . I failed utterly to pass the entrance examination, though it seemed even at that time to be easy. I think I was bewildered. I returned to the office and handed Mr. Curtis the note, which announced it. He, too, seemed very much disappointed. . . . He passed the note to Mr. F. C. Briggs, then the business agent of Hampton Institute, who sat at a desk near him. The two whispered some words. . . . Mr. Briggs remarked . . . in an under-tone to Mr. Curtis, . . . 'I think you had better keep him if you can.' Mr. Curtis then turned to me with the words, 'Well, young man, what are you going to do?' I told him that I had come to stay at any cost . . .

"He wanted to know if I had any objection to hard work. I assured him I was not afraid of hard work, that I had worked hard all my life. . . . I preferred the saw-mill, and was so assigned. Later I was transferred from piling lumber to a raft of logs in the creek. . . . I was shown how to perform this operation by another Virginia boy by the name of John H. Palmer. . . . I was impressed by his kindness and patience."

—Robert Russa Moton, Hampton, Class of 1889

ON THE SIDE

Side dishes are to meal presentation what accessories are to decorating. They should compliment the main dish as to color and sometimes contrast with it as to texture and temperature. In this way you enhance the visual appeal of the meal, adding to everyone's enjoyment.

—C.Q.T.

COWPEAS

A Hampton Heritage Recipe, from Carrie Alberta Lyford,
director of the Home Economics School at the Hampton Normal and Agricultural Institute

"Cowpeas should be Cooked soon after gathering, in order to preserve their fine flavor. Cook the green cowpeas (in pod or shelled) in boiling salted water until tender. Season and serve. Dried cowpeas should be soaked overnight (7 or 8 hours) then boiled until tender. By absorbing water, dried cowpeas increase in size until each cup makes nearly 2½ cups of cooked beans."

BOSTON BAKED BEANS

A Hampton Heritage Recipe, from Carrie Alberta Lyford,
director of the Home Economics School at the Hampton Normal and Agricultural Institute

1	quart navy beans	3	tablespoons sugar
½	pound fat salt pork	2	tablespoons molasses
1	tablespoon salt		Boiling water
1½	teaspoons dry mustard		

Pick over the beans and soak them in cold water overnight. In the morning, drain them, cover with fresh water, and heat slowly until the skins burst, but do not let the beans become broken!

Scald ½ pound of fat salt pork, scrape it, and put a slice in the bottom of the bean pot. Cut the remaining pork across the top in strips just through the rind and bury the pork in the beans, leaving the rind exposed.

Add 1 cup of the boiling water to the flavorings and pour over the beans. Cover with boiling water. Bake slowly, adding more water as necessary. Bake at 250 degrees F. for 6 to 8 hours; uncover at the last so that the water will evaporate and the beans will brown on top.

12 servings

William T. Fuller, a member of Hampton's class of '91, graduated from Leonard Medical School at Shaw University and went on to practice medicine in Suffolk, Virginia. Writing to Myrtilla J. Sherman on Christmas Day of 1912, Fuller reminisced, ". . . the thing that stands out most prominent in the Hampton boys' minds, is what we called 'Bean morning.' No boy or girl ever remained from the dining room on 'Bean morning' even the most laggard would be on time for this meal. . . . Although it has been more than twenty-one years since I have left Hampton, where ever I have met a Hampton boy and had an opportunity to talk with him of old Hampton days 'Bean morning' has always been a part of the conversation." In physiology, one of the activities is preparation of a cheap, hygienic bill of fare for breakfast, dinner, and tea. These bills of fare were inspired by the New England movement. A cook was sent to be trained at the cooking school of Miss Parloa in Boston. Thus the Boston Baked Beans. (This writer found "Chicken Thursday" at the Holly Tree Inn to be exceptional.)

PINTO BEANS

1 pound dried pinto beans	1 teaspoon onion powder
1 large onion, chopped	1 teaspoon garlic powder
¼ cup bacon drippings	¾ teaspoon seasoned salt
1 ham hock or smoked turkey wing, washed	

Place the beans in a large colander. Remove any foreign objects, then wash the beans under cold running water. Next, place the beans in a large bowl and add sufficient water to cover by 3 inches. Soak the beans overnight. Drain before cooking. In a large pot, over medium heat, sauté the onion in the bacon drippings. Add the meat to the pot, along with enough water to cover. Bring to a rapid boil, reduce the heat, and simmer for 1 hour. Add the beans and, if required, additional water to cover beans. Place a lid on the pot and simmer for approximately 1 hour. Add the seasonings, stir, and cook for an additional hour or until the beans are tender. Remove the lid during the last 15 to 30 minutes of cooking and allow the beans to "cook down" until the broth reaches the desired consistency. Add additional seasonings if desired.

6 to 8 servings

BAKED PINTO BEANS

These beans are very popular at barbecues, picnics and pot-luck dinners where the invitation includes a request for "those wonderful beans." Even when I am unavailable, I am asked to please send the beans anyway.

2	cups dried pinto beans	2	tablespoons tomato paste
1	medium onion, chopped	½	cup molasses
1	cup stewed tomatoes, chopped	2	teaspoons dry mustard
		1	tablespoon chili powder

Pick over the beans to remove any foreign objects and soak them overnight in enough water to cover by 3 inches. Drain and rinse the beans. Preheat the oven to 250 degrees F. Place the beans and remaining ingredients in a casserole. Add boiling water to barely cover the beans and top the casserole with a tight-fitting lid. Bake for 4 to 5 hours, or until tender. Add additional water as necessary to keep the beans sufficiently moist. Uncover the casserole and let the beans cook for 30 minutes longer without adding more water.

4 servings

SOUTHERN CORN BREAD DRESSING

3	slices white bread	1	teaspoon dried basil
1	pan J. R.'s Skillet Corn Bread (see page 181)	1	teaspoon dried marjoram
1	tablespoon white vinegar	2	teaspoons garlic powder
1	cup milk	2	teaspoons onion powder
½	cup (1 stick) butter	1	tablespoon coarsely ground black pepper
1½	cups chopped onion	2	teaspoons seasoned salt
2	cups chopped celery	1	large egg, slightly beaten
1¼	cups chopped green bell pepper	2	cups chicken broth
1	tablespoon ground sage	¼	cup bacon drippings or vegetable oil
2	teaspoons dried thyme	4	hard-boiled eggs, chopped

Preheat the oven to 350 degrees F. Place the sliced bread and corn bread in a large bowl. Add the vinegar to the milk, pour over the bread, and set aside. In a large skillet, melt the butter and sauté the onion, celery, and green pepper until tender but not mushy. Remove from the heat. Combine the next eight seasoning ingredients, mix well, and spoon into the bowl with the bread mixture. Add the remaining ingredients, mix well, and pour into a well-greased casserole pan. Place in the preheated oven and bake for 1 hour or as long as necessary to obtain a crusty exterior and soft but firm interior.

8 to 10 servings

New Potatoes With Chives

These delicious potatoes bring to mind my grandmother's wonderful "kitchen door garden," where, within yards of her large country kitchen, she grew the the most delicious vegetables . . . including new potatoes.

24	small red potatoes, about 2 inches in diameter	¼	cup (½ stick) butter, melted
		1½	tablespoons snipped fresh chives

Place the potatoes in a large pot with sufficient cold water to cover by 2 inches. Bring to a slow boil and simmer for 10 minutes or until tender. Drain the potatoes and return them to the pot. Allow the potatoes to steam over low heat for 1 minute, shaking the pot gently to prevent them from sticking and burning. Cool the potatoes, quarter them, and arrange in a shallow serving dish. Drizzle the butter over the potatoes, coating evenly; season, gently mix, and sprinkle with chives just prior to serving.

4 to 6 servings

Sunday Services

". . . I remember so well my first Sunday night at Hampton. Six hundred or more students . . . assembled for evening prayers. . . . In [a] simple yet inspiring prayer, Mr. Frissell . . . asked God's blessing upon the humble mothers and fathers in all of the homes represented by the young people before him, the poorest as well as the best. . . . [Mr. Frissell] prayed that, amid the pleasant surroundings of Hampton Institute, the young people would always remember their parents who did not live, all of them, in such an environment as we had at Hampton. . . .

"It seemed most strange to me, amid [Hampton's] new surroundings and so many new faces, that everybody should turn aside from work and study, and that this gentleman, a stranger to me, should be thinking, as I supposed, about my old mother, and that he should put in such beautiful words the very thoughts and feelings which were in my own mind. . . . During Sunday services, I, expected to hear regular church music such as would be sung by white people mostly, and such as was written as I supposed by white people also. I had come to school to learn to do things differently; to sing, to speak, and to use the language, and of course, the music, not of coloured people. . . .

"The students sang plantation songs, the religious folk songs of the Negro. I had been brought up on this kind of music . . . but somehow there was something about this singing—with the four parts blending almost as if there were just one great voice singing, that almost carried me into a new world. . . . I had never heard such singing, but somehow, notwithstanding my thorough enjoyment of the music, the dress, and manner of the pupils, and my real appreciation of being in such a wonderful institution, I was disappointed to hear these songs sung by educated people and in an educational institution. . . .

". . . One or two of the older students argued that the songs were beautiful and people enjoyed them so why should we not sing them. The only reply I could give was that they were Negro songs and that we had come to Hampton to learn something better. . . . In later years, Moton would recall that as a young child he had been made to feel ashamed of plantation songs when minstrel show singers parodied the songs to ridicule his race.

"A few Sunday evenings later, when General Armstrong had returned to the Institute, he spoke in his own forceful manner to the students about respecting themselves, their race, their history, their traditions, their songs, and folk lore in general. He referred then to the Negro songs as 'a priceless legacy,' which he hoped [would] always [be cherished]. . . .

—Robert Russa Moton, Hampton, Class of 1889

"I was impressed with [General Armstrong] and his address . . . but . . . not entirely convinced. However, I was led to think along a little different line regarding my race. The truth is it was the first time I had ever given any thought to race. . . . The time at Hampton, was also the first time in my life that I had begun to think that there was anything that the Negro had that was deserving of consideration."

—Robert Russa Moton, Hampton, Class of 1889

Perhaps because of his Hampton experiences or maybe due to the African studies program implemented by General Armstrong and evident as early as the 1870's, Moton would in his later memoir recall his heritage with pride.

According to Dr. Moton, . . . In approximately 1735, a slave ship, "arrived at the shores of America; the human cargo was brought to Richmond and . . . sold at public auction in the slave markets of the city. Among those sold was one who was bought by a tobacco planter and carried to Amelia County, Virginia, where he lived to be a very old man. This man was my grandmother's great-grandfather. . . . According to my grandmother, [my great, great, great-grandfather]. . . . learned very little English and . . . never grew to like America. . . . Certain days . . . he observed religiously throughout his life. These were feast days with certain ceremonies of their own. . . . When possible, two other members of that same party though not of his tribe would join him. . . .

"My mother, like her own mother, was a woman of very strong character in many ways, very much like my father. Among my early recollections is the fact that my mother frequently, after working in the field all day, would hurry us through the evening meal in order to get the cabin ready for the night school which met regularly in our simple home. . . . I recall now the eagerness with which some twenty-five or thirty men and women struggled with their lessons, trying to learn to read and write while I was supposed to be asleep in my trundle bed, to which I had been hurried to make room for this little band of anxious, aspiring ex-slaves, some of whom came as far as six miles in order to take advantage of this rare opportunity which but a few years before had been denied them. . . ."

—Robert Russa Moton, Hampton, Class of 1889

The first generation of Hampton graduates learned to take pride in the freedom of self-reliance and self-determination. The second generation, those not born in bondage, learned to take pride in the accomplishments of the generations that went before them. They learned to cherish the history, traditions, culture, and music of a bound people, which expressed their faith that one day they would be free. It expressed their belief that freedom would necessarily include a free and equal right to fully participate in a democratic society, live in peace and harmony with those of every race, creed, and color and achieve the loftiest of goals—limited only by their talent and determination to achieve.

"Thinking of the experiences through which my ancestors passed, along with thousands of other slaves, I have often felt that somehow—in spite of the hardships and oppression which they suffered—that in the providence of God, the Negro . . . has come through the ordeal with much to his credit. . . .

"While I learned many valuable lessons from books during this first year, they were insignificant as compared with the indescribable something which I gathered outside of books, very real at Hampton, and very real to me, too, which I cannot accurately describe in writing, but which was nevertheless very pronounced and very definite. . . .

—Robert Russa Moton, Hampton, Class of 1889

CREAMED MASHED POTATOES

7	medium russet baking potatoes	6	tablespoons (¾ stick) butter
½	cup heavy cream		Salt and black pepper to taste

Wash the potatoes and place them in a pot of boiling water deep enough to cover them by at least 3 inches and permit them to boil freely. Bring the potatoes to a second boil; reduce the heat to medium low and simmer for approximately 1 hour. When done, drain the water from the potatoes. Return the pot to the burner, cover, and steam for an additional 30 seconds or until dry. Allow the potatoes to cool until they can be handled without burning. Remove the skins, place the pulp in a warmed serving bowl, and mash in the cream and butter. Add additional butter, cream, or seasoning to taste.

6 to 8 servings

SWEET POTATOES IN ORANGE CUPS

4   large navel oranges, halved,
      with seeds and pulp
      removed (reserve cups)
1   tablespoon butter
1   tablespoon orange juice
4   large sweet potatoes, boiled,
      peeled, and mashed
      (1½ cups)

1   egg
2   tablespoons light brown sugar
½   teaspoon orange zest
⅛   teaspoon ground nutmeg
¼   teaspoon ground cinnamon
2   tablespoons finely chopped pecans

Preheat the oven to 350 degrees F. Set the prepared orange cups side by side in a baking dish. In a large mixing bowl, combine the pulp, butter, orange juice, and mashed sweet potatoes. Add the egg, sugar, orange zest, and spices. Fill each orange cup with the mixture by swirling it in attractively or piping it in using a pastry bag and decorative tip. Sprinkle with the pecan pieces, place in the oven, and bake for 45 minutes or until the tops are lightly browned.

4 servings

SWEET POTATO SOUFFLÉ

4   pounds sweet potatoes, cut in
      pieces
½   cup (1 stick) softened
      unsalted butter, cut in
      pieces
½   cup granulated sugar
½   cup light brown sugar
4   large eggs
3   tablespoons self-rising flour

1   cup light cream
¼   teaspoon salt
1   teaspoon vanilla extract
½   cup chopped pecans
2   tablespoons firmly packed dark
      brown sugar
¼   teaspoon ground cinnamon
¼   teaspoon ground allspice
⅛   teaspoon ground nutmeg

In a large pot, combine the potatoes and sufficient water to cover them by 2 inches. Bring the water to a boil, and boil for 30 to 45 minutes or until the potatoes are fork-tender. Preheat the oven to 350 degrees F. Drain the potatoes, allow to cool until they are readily handled, then remove and discard the potato skins. Place the peeled potatoes in a large bowl. With an electric mixer, beat the potatoes until smooth; then beat in the butter, sugars, eggs (one at a time), flour, cream, salt, and vanilla until well combined. Divide between two 1½-quart soufflé dishes. In a separate small bowl, combine the pecans, dark brown sugar, and spices; mix well. Sprinkle the mixture on top of the soufflés. Bake in the middle of the oven for 1 hour.

10 to 12 servings

CANDIED YAMS

8	small sweet potatoes, peeled and quartered	½	teaspoon salt	
1½	tablespoons fresh lemon juice	1	teaspoon grated lemon rind	
½	cup butter	⅛	teaspoon ground ginger	
¾	cup brown sugar	¼	teaspoon ground cinnamon	
		1	teaspoon ground nutmeg	

Cook the potatoes in boiling water to cover, along with the lemon juice, until they're fork-tender. When done, remove the potatoes from the pot and drain. In the same pot, over medium heat, melt the butter and sugar. Stirring constantly, continue to cook until the sugar melts and begins to bubble. When the mixture begins to thicken, remove it from the heat, add the salt, grated lemon rind, and the spices, and return the potatoes to pot, coating them with the mixture. Serve immediately or transfer to a buttered glass baking dish and keep in a warm oven until ready to serve.

4 to 6 servings

TWICE-BAKED SWEET POTATO DELIGHT

4	small unpeeled sweet potatoes		½	teaspoon ground cinnamon
2½	tablespoons butter		½	teaspoon ground allspice
½	cup golden raisins		1	8-ounce can unsweetened pineapple, drained
2½	tablespoons brown sugar		2	tablespoons chopped pecans

Place the potatoes on a baking sheet. Bake in a preheated 400-degree F. oven for 1 hour or until done. Allow the potatoes to cool for 15 minutes. Cut each potato in half lengthwise and scoop the pulp into a bowl, leaving the shells intact. Mash the pulp and butter together. Stir in the remaining ingredients, except pecans. Spoon the mixture into the shells and sprinkle with pecans. Bake for 15 minutes.

4 servings

HOMEMADE CRANBERRY CUPS

1	pound cranberries, picked over, washed, and destemmed		1	cup orange juice
			½	cup granulated sugar
4	oranges, halved, with seeds and pulp removed (reserve cups)		½	cup light brown sugar
			1	teaspoon orange zest
			¾	teaspoon ground allspice
			1¼	teaspoons ground cinnamon

Prepare the cranberries and set aside. Combine the juice and sugars in a heavy medium saucepan. Bring to a boil over high heat, stirring, until the sugar dissolves. Add the cranberries and cook, stirring often, until the berries begin to pop, approximately 7 minutes. Remove from the heat and add the remaining ingredients. Cool completely, cover, and refrigerate until chilled and set, approximately 2 hours. Fill the cups with this mixture just prior to serving. The cranberry sauce may be made up to 3 days in advance.

8 servings

School assembly
(Reproduced from the collections of the Library of Congress)

A Legend Returns to Hampton

"In his introduction, General Armstrong said 'Booker Washington . . . had served as his private secretary, and that he had recommended him for the work in Alabama—That during the past five years he had wonderful success in gaining the good will of the people surrounding the Institute and that the North had responded to his appeals for aid. . . .' Indeed General . . . Armstrong pointed [Booker T. Washington] out as a sample of what he hoped the Hampton students would look forward to becoming after completing their education. He hoped they would start schools on the Hampton plan in rural communities.

"[Mr. Washington] spoke of what he was trying to do at Tuskegee Institute and said, modestly, that he was trying to carry out, as any graduate should do, the ideas of General

Armstrong and Hampton. He spoke clearly of the importance and value of trade education and while he did not . . . belittle college education, he did emphasize the fundamental
need of trade education, the buying of land, the building of homes, bank accounts, etc.
These, he declared, were essential to the highest development of any people. As I think
of it now, and as I thought of it then, we considered it perhaps the most remarkable address
we had ever heard, and coming from a coloured man . . . it was all the more impressive.

"We were not expected to applaud in chapel at Sunday evening services, but there
was a spontaneous outburst of applause from the audience when [Booker T. Washington]
sat down, and it was prolonged. General Armstrong arose, remarking, 'I am glad you had
the good sense to break the rule on such an occasion' and added, 'This is for me as well
as for you a very happy hour.' It is unnecessary to remark that [Washington's] address was
the talk of the year among the students and teachers.

"We had some Indian friends who used to come to our rooms after meetings of this
sort. I recall now that until 'taps,' some eight or ten of us, with our Indian friends, dis-
cussed that speech. One of the latter, John Archambeau, remarked to the group that the
only fault he found with Booker T. Washington was the fact that he was not an Indian."

—Robert Russa Moton, Hampton, Class of 1889

CORN CUSTARD

1 cup fresh corn kernels, chopped coarse
1 tablespoon grated onion
1 teaspoon salt
2¾ cups half-and-half, divided
1 cup yellow cornmeal

½ cup (1 stick) unsalted butter, equally divided into 1-inch pieces
3 eggs, separated, at room temperature
2 teaspoons sugar
¼ teaspoon ground nutmeg
4 bacon strips, fried crisp

Preheat the oven to 400 degrees F. Butter a 2-quart soufflé dish. Combine the corn kernels, grated onion, salt, and 2 cups of the half-and-half in a medium saucepan; bring to a boil over high heat and stir until very thick, approximately 1 minute. Remove the saucepan from the heat. Immediately beat in the cornmeal and butter, one piece at a time. Stir in the remaining ¾ cup of half-and-half. Blend in the yolks one at a time. Add the sugar and nutmeg. Beat the egg whites until stiff but not dry. Fold one-quarter of the whites into the cornmeal mixture, then fold in the remaining whites, blending gently but thoroughly. Pour into the prepared soufflé dish. Bake for 10 minutes. Reduce the oven temperature to 375 degrees. Continue cooking until the custard puffs and browns, but the center is still soft, about 55 minutes. Crumble the bacon over the custard for garnish. Serve hot.

6 to 8 servings

CORN CHOWDER

*A Hampton Heritage Recipe, from Carrie Alberta Lyford,
director of the Home Economics School at the Hampton Normal and Agricultural Institute*

1 small onion
3 tablespoons butter or margarine
1 [12½-ounce] can corn
Sliced potato [about 3 medium potatoes, peeled and sliced]

1 quart water
1 tablespoon flour
1 teaspoon salt
¼ teaspoon black pepper
1½ cups milk
¼ can tomatoes or four fresh tomatoes
⅛ teaspoon baking soda

Cut the onion very fine and brown slightly in 2 tablespoons of fat. Put alternate layers of sliced potato and corn in a kettle. Add the onion, cover with water, and simmer until tender. Make a white sauce of 1 tablespoon fat, flour, seasonings, and milk; add the white sauce to the chowder. Cook for 5 to 10 minutes.

Cook the tomatoes and strain. Just before serving, add the soda to the tomatoes, then add the tomatoes to the chowder.

8 to 10 servings

WILD RICE TIMBALES

¼ cup finely chopped onion	3 tablespoons unsalted butter
¼ cup finely chopped green onions, including tops	2 cups wild rice
¼ cup finely chopped celery	4 cups chicken broth
1 large garlic clove, minced	Salt and black pepper to taste

In a large, heavy saucepan, sauté the onions, celery, and garlic in the butter over medium-low heat until the onions are transparent. Stir in the rice. Cook the rice while stirring constantly for approximately 1 minute. Add the chicken broth and bring to a boil. Reduce the heat, cover, and simmer for approximately 45 minutes. Remove the saucepan from the heat and allow to stand undisturbed for 15 minutes. Fluff the rice, add salt and pepper to taste, and divide rice equally among eight ½-cup timbales. Press the rice firmly into the timbales to mold and then invert onto a serving platter or plate.

8 servings

RICE PILAF WITH CARAMELIZED ONIONS

⅔ cup minced onion	3 cups water
¼ cup vegetable oil	1½ teaspoons salt
1½ cups long-grain rice	½ cup baby green peas
(not converted)	

In a large, heavy saucepan, cook the onion in the oil over moderate heat, stirring, until it is golden brown. Add the rice and cook the mixture, stirring, until the rice begins to brown. Add the water and salt; bring to a boil. Continue to boil, uncovered, over medium-high heat for 7 to 10 minutes, or until the surface of the rice is clearly visible. Reduce the heat to low, gently stir in the peas, and cook the rice, covered, for 10 minutes, or until it is tender and the liquid is absorbed. Fluff the rice with a fork, remove from the heat, and let it stand, covered, for about 5 minutes.

6 to 8 servings

HAM RICE PILAF

2 tablespoons bacon drippings	½ cup chopped ham
½ cup finely chopped onion	1 cup rice
¼ cup chopped green bell	2¼ cups beef broth
pepper	½ teaspoon seasoned salt
1 garlic clove, minced	¼ teaspoon onion powder

In a large saucepan over medium-high heat, sauté the onion and bell pepper in bacon drippings until the onion is soft and golden. Add the garlic and ham, and sauté for 1 or 2 minutes more. Add the rice and cook, stirring constantly, until the rice is shiny and translucent. In a separate saucepan, bring the stock to a boil. Pour over the rice and bring to a second boil. Add the seasoned salt and onion powder, cover, and cook for an additional 20 to 25 minutes.

4 to 6 servings

WILD RICE STUFFING

2	cups uncooked wild rice	⅓	cup minced celery
4	cups chicken broth	1½	cups sliced fresh mushrooms
½	cup (1 stick) butter	1	teaspoon salt
1	small yellow onion, chopped fine	¼	teaspoon ground black pepper
1	cup sliced green onions	3	tablespoons sherry

Prepare the wild rice according to the package directions, but substitute broth for the water. In a medium saucepan over medium heat, sauté the remaining ingredients, except the sherry, in the butter. In a large mixing bowl, combine the rice with the contents of the saucepan. Add the sherry and additional seasonings to taste. Use the mixture to stuff pheasant or other fowl; any excess can be served as a side dish.

4 to 6 servings

PECAN STUFFING

½	cup (1 stick) butter, divided	½	teaspoon onion powder
1	onion, minced	¼	teaspoon garlic powder
½	pound fresh mushrooms, chopped	½	teaspoon ground nutmeg
8	slices white bread, toasted	½	cup seedless raisins
1	teaspoon salt	¼	teaspoon mace
½	teaspoon ground black pepper	6	hard-boiled eggs
		2	cups pecans, chopped
		½	cup dry sherry

In a large saucepan, melt half of the butter and sauté the onion until soft. Add the mushrooms and cook until the onion is translucent. Crush the toast to fine crumbs and combine with the spices. Melt the remaining butter in the pan, then add the toast crumbs and remaining ingredients. Mix well. This makes enough stuffing for a 12- to 15-pound turkey. Do not overstuff. Place any excess dressing in a baking pan and bake the last half hour.

4 to 6 servings

BREADS AND BISCUITS

Dinah Kneading Dough

I have seen full many a sight

born of day or drawn by night;

Sunlight on a silver stream,

Golden lilies all a-dream,

Lofty mountains, bold and proud

Veiled beneath the lacelike cloud;

But no lovely sight I know

Equals Dinah kneading dough.

—Paul Laurence Dunbar
from "At Candlelightin' Time"

Dinah kneading dough
(Private collection, Carolyn Quick Tillery)

BUTTERMILK ROLLS

1	teaspoon sugar	¼	cup sugar
½	cup warm water	1	teaspoon baking soda
3	packages yeast	1	cup (2 sticks) butter
5	cups self-rising flour	2	cups warm buttermilk

Add the sugar to the warm water and dissolve the yeast in the mixture; set aside. In a large mixing bowl, combine the flour, remaining sugar, and baking soda. Cut in the butter until the mixture resembles coarse meal. Stir in the yeast mixture and buttermilk, mixing well. Turn out onto a lightly floured surface and knead lightly a few times. Roll to a ½-inch thickness. Cut with a floured biscuit cutter, then dip each biscuit into melted butter and place on a cookie sheet. Cover and let rise for approximately 1 hour. Bake at 400 degrees F. for 10 minutes.

Yields approximately 12 rolls

POTATO YEAST ROLLS

2	packages dry yeast	½	cup shortening
½	cup lukewarm water	2	tablespoons honey
1	cup hot water	1	cup mashed potatoes
1	tablespoon salt	2	eggs, lightly beaten
½	cup sugar	6–7	cups flour

Dissolve the yeast in the lukewarm water and set aside. In a large bowl, combine the hot water, salt, sugar, shortening, honey, and potatoes. Cool and add the yeast mixture, eggs, and 1½ cups of the flour. Cover and allow to rise for 1½ hours. Add enough of the remaining flour to make a soft dough. Knead well and allow to rise for about 2 hours. Shape into rolls and let rise for an additional 2 hours. Bake for 20 to 25 minutes at 350 degrees F.

Yields 12 rolls

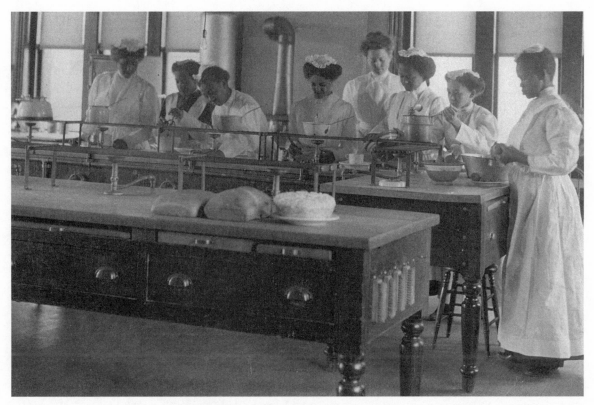

Hampton ladies baking and cooking
(Courtesy of Hampton University Archives)

POTATO ROLLS

Make a second pan! These light, fluffy, melt-in-your-mouth rolls will quickly disappear from the table.

2	cups water	1	cup instant potato flakes
1	cup milk	¼	cup honey
½	cup butter-flavored solid shortening	2	teaspoons salt
7–8	cups flour	2	tablespoons yeast

Warm the milk, water, and shortening. Add to the dry ingredients. Knead. Cover and allow to rise until doubled (approximately 1 hour). Punch down. Allow to rise a second time. Shape rolls, and let them rise. Bake at 375 degrees F. for approximately 18 minutes.

Yields approximately 12 rolls

FRIED BISCUITS

1 cup all-purpose flour
2 teaspoons double-acting
  baking powder
1 teaspoon salt
2 tablespoons butter, cut into
  pieces

2 tablespoons half-and-half
¼ cup milk
1½ pounds (3 cups) solid shortening,
  for frying

Combine the flour, baking powder, and salt; sift into a large bowl. Add the butter and rub together until the mixture resembles coarse meal. Mix together the half-and-half and milk, and add to the flour mixture. Toss lightly with fingers or a fork, taking care not to overwork the dough. Gather into a ball and place on a lightly floured surface. Roll to a thickness of approximately ¼ inch. Cut with a biscuit cutter to form 1½-inch rounds. Collect the scraps and form a ball, roll them out again, and cut as many rounds as possible from the remaining dough. Melt the shortening into a large, heavy, cast-iron skillet. Heat the shortening until it is very hot but not smoking (approximately 375 degrees F.). Fry the biscuits for about 4 or 5 minutes, turning until they are evenly browned on both sides. Remove to a paper-towel-lined plate to drain. Serve with chicken and gravy, covering the biscuits with gravy.

Yields approximately 12 biscuits

PEPPERED BUTTERMILK BISCUITS

3¾ cups unbleached all-purpose
     flour
2   tablespoons baking powder
2   teaspoons freshly ground
     pepper

1¼ teaspoons salt
6   tablespoons (¾ stick) unsalted butter
⅓   cup solid vegetable shortening
1   cup chilled buttermilk
½   cup chilled half-and-half

Preheat the oven to 450 degrees F. In a large bowl, mix together the first four ingredients. Cut the butter and shortening into pieces, add to the flour, and rub them into the flour with your fingertips until coarse crumbs form. Mix in the buttermilk and half-and-half to form a soft dough. Turn the dough out onto a floured surface and gently knead until combined, about half a minute. With a rolling pin, roll the dough to a thickness of ½ inch. Cut out biscuits, using a standard cutter. Place the biscuits on an ungreased cookie sheet and bake until golden, approximately 15 minutes.

Yields approximately 12 biscuits

SWEET POTATO BISCUITS

¾   cup mashed cooked sweet
     potatoes
¼   cup melted butter
1   tablespoon honey
⅔   cup half-and-half

1¼ cups flour
4   teaspoons baking powder
1   tablespoon brown sugar
½   teaspoon salt
⅛   teaspoon ground nutmeg

Preheat the oven to 450 degrees F. Mix together the potatoes, butter, and honey. Add the half-and-half, then sift together the remaining ingredients and add them to the sweet potato mixture to form a soft dough. Turn out on a floured board and knead very lightly five times, or until the outside looks smooth. Roll out to a ½-inch thickness. Cut biscuits and place them ½ inch apart on an ungreased baking sheet. Bake in the preheated oven for 20 minutes. Serve warm.

Yields approximately 12 biscuits

SOUP STICKS

A Hampton Heritage Recipe, from Carrie Alberta Lyford,
director of the Home Economics School at the Hampton Normal and Agricultural Institute

"Cut stale bread into ⅓-inch slices, remove crusts, then butter and cut into ⅓-inch strips, brown in oven."

BUTTERMILK BISCUITS

2	cups all-purpose flour		½	teaspoon salt
2	teaspoons baking powder		⅓	cup solid shortening
¼	teaspoon baking soda		¾	cup buttermilk

Preheat the oven to 450 degrees F. In a large bowl, combine the first four ingredients. Using a fork or pastry blender, cut in the shortening until the mixture resembles coarse cornmeal. Blend in the buttermilk until a soft dough is formed. Turn out onto a lightly floured surface and lightly knead seven or eight times. Roll out to a ½-inch thickness and cut out with a floured biscuit cutter. Place the biscuits on an ungreased cookie sheet about 1 inch apart and bake until golden, about 15 minutes.

Yields 12 to 18 biscuits, depending on the size cutter used

BAKING POWDER BISCUITS

2	cups all-purpose flour		2	teaspoons salt
3¼	teaspoons baking powder		¼	cup shortening
½	teaspoon sugar		¾	cup half-and-half

Preheat the oven to 450 degrees F. In a large bowl, sift together the dry ingredients. Cut in the shortening. Add the half-and-half and stir until a soft dough is formed. Knead gently several times before rolling out to a ½-inch thickness on a lightly floured surface. Cut with a biscuit cutter, and prick the top of each biscuit with a fork. Bake in the preheated oven for 12 to 15 minutes. Serve hot.

Yields 12 to 18 biscuits, depending on the size cutter used

J. R.'S SKILLET CORN BREAD

½	cup all-purpose flour		1	cup whole milk
1	cup yellow cornmeal		1	egg, beaten
¼	cup sugar		¼	cup vegetable oil
1½	teaspoons baking powder		¼	teaspoon salt (optional)

Preheat the oven to 425 degrees F. Mix dry ingredients in a large bowl. Slowly add the milk, beaten egg, and vegetable oil, and mix well; set aside. Pour the oil into a 10-inch cast-iron skillet, and place it in the preheated oven for approximately 10 minutes (oil should start to smoke). Remove skillet from the oven and carefully pour in the batter. Reduce oven heat to 400 degrees and bake for 20 to 25 minutes. Remove bread from oven and brown under broiler, if necessary. Turn out onto an ovenproof plate and serve hot with butter.

8 to 10 servings

Booker T. Washington
(Courtesy of Hampton University Archives)

PAN BREAD

½ cup flour
1½ teaspoons salt
1 tablespoon baking powder
1½ cups cornmeal
3 eggs

¾ cup milk
1 tablespoon sugar
¼ cup melted bacon drippings or
    shortening

Preheat the oven to 400 degrees F. Sift together the flour, salt, and baking powder into a bowl. Add the cornmeal and mix well. Add the eggs, milk, sugar, and melted drippings or shortening. Beat until smooth. Pour into a hot, greased, 8-inch square baking pan. Bake for about 20 to 25 minutes.

12 servings

HUSH PUPPIES

½ cup stone-ground cornmeal
½ cup all-purpose flour
1 teaspoon double-acting
    baking powder
½ teaspoon salt
3 tablespoons chopped onion
2 teaspoons sugar

½ teaspoon onion powder
¼ teaspoon garlic powder
¼ teaspoon cayenne pepper
1 egg
¾ cup milk
   Oil for deep frying

Combine the dry ingredients and set aside. In a separate bowl, combine the egg and milk; mix well. Next, combine the milk mixture with the dry ingredients; form into oblong cakes and deep-fry at 370 degrees F. until golden.

4 servings

CORN MUFFINS

1 cup cornmeal	1 cup half-and-half
½ cup all-purpose flour	2 well-beaten eggs
1 tablespoon baking powder	2 tablespoons honey
⅛ teaspoon ground nutmeg	3 tablespoons melted butter
¾ teaspoon salt	

Preheat the oven to 350 degrees F. Line twelve muffin cups with paper liners. Put the cornmeal in a mixing bowl; sift in the flour, baking powder, nutmeg, and salt. Add the half-and-half, eggs, honey, and butter. Mix well and spoon into the paper-lined muffin cups. Bake for 20 minutes or until golden.

Yields 1 dozen muffins

Young men training in woodworking
(Reproduced from the collections of the Library of Congress)

SWEET POTATO AND MOLASSES MUFFINS

1	large sweet potato, cooked until tender and peeled	1¼	cups all-purpose flour	
2	eggs, lightly beaten	½	cup whole-wheat flour	
¼	cup half-and-half	2	teaspoons baking powder	
¼	cup milk	1	teaspoon ground cinnamon	
½	cup molasses	½	teaspoon ground ginger	
3	tablespoons butter, melted	⅛	teaspoon ground nutmeg	
		¾	teaspoon salt	

Preheat the oven to 400 degrees F. Line twelve large muffin cups with foil muffin papers. Purée the potato. Measure 1 cup of the purée and transfer to a mixing bowl. Mix in the eggs, half-and-half, milk, molasses, and butter. Add all the remaining ingredients and stir just until mixed. Fill the cups. Bake until springy to the touch and a tester inserted into the center comes out with just a few moist crumbs—about 25 minutes. Serve warm.

Yields 12 muffins

HONEYED SWEET POTATO MUFFINS

For a delicious breakfast treat, serve any leftover muffins for breakfast by crumbling them into a bowl, adding butter, honey, and cream. Warm in the microwave and garnish with toasted sunflower seeds.

1	large orange-fleshed sweet potato (about ¼ pound), cooked	1¼	cups all-purpose flour	
2	eggs, well beaten	½	cup whole-wheat flour	
½	cup light cream	2	teaspoons baking powder	
½	cup honey	1	teaspoon ground cinnamon	
¼	cup (½ stick) butter, melted	¼	teaspoon ground nutmeg	
2	tablespoons light brown sugar	⅛	teaspoon ground allspice	
		¾	teaspoon salt	

Preheat the oven to 400 degrees F. Line twelve large muffin tins with foil muffin papers. Purée the potato and transfer 1 cup of purée to a mixing bowl. Mix in the eggs, cream, honey, and butter. Add the remaining ingredients and gently stir until just mixed. Pour the batter into the prepared muffin cups. Bake for 20 or 25 minutes, or until springy to the touch and a tester inserted in the middle of a muffin comes out clean. Serve hot with butter or honey.

Yields 12 muffins

Young men training in wheel wrighting
(Reproduced from the collections of the Library of Congress)

SWEET POTATO BREAD

- 5¼ cups flour
- 1 tablespoon baking soda
- 1 tablespoon ground cinnamon
- 1 tablespoon ground nutmeg
- 1 tablespoon ground allspice
- 2¼ teaspoons salt
- 2 cups brown sugar
- 2 cups granulated sugar
- 1½ cups vegetable oil
- 6 eggs
- 1½ cups pineapple juice
- 3 cups cooked mashed sweet potato
- ½ cup heavy cream
- 2 teaspoons vanilla extract
- ½ cup golden raisins
- ¾ cup halved pecans

In a large bowl, combine the first six ingredients and set aside. In a separate bowl, combine the sugars, oil, eggs, pineapple juice, and sweet potatoes. Add the flour mixture and beat together; stir in the heavy cream, vanilla extract, raisins, and pecans. Pour into three 7⅝ × 3⅝ × 2¼ loaf pans. Bake at 325 degrees F. for 1¼ to 1½ hours or until a toothpick comes out clean when inserted in the middle of the bread.

Yields 3 loaves

STRAWBERRY BREAD

- 3 cups all-purpose flour
- 1 teaspoon baking powder
- 1 teaspoon salt
- 1 tablespoon ground cinnamon
- 2 cups sugar
- 2¼ cups sliced strawberries
- 4 eggs, well beaten
- ½ cup melted butter
- 1 cup vegetable oil
- 1 cup chopped pecans

Preheat the oven to 350 degrees F. In a large bowl, sift together the dry ingredients. Make a deep well in the center. In a separate bowl, combine the remaining ingredients, mix well, and pour into the flour well. Stir just enough to moisten all ingredients. Pour into two greased and floured loaf pans. Bake for 1 hour.

Yields 2 loaves

BLACK WALNUT BREAD

3	cups sifted all-purpose flour		2	eggs
4½	teaspoons baking powder		1	cup light cream
¼	cup sugar		2	tablespoons honey
¼	cup brown sugar		¼	cup melted butter
¾	teaspoon salt		1	cup chopped black walnuts

Sift together the flour, baking powder, sugars, and salt into a mixing bowl. Beat together the eggs, cream, honey, and melted butter. Add the flour mixture and the walnuts; stir until thoroughly blended but slightly lumpy. Spoon into a lightly greased 8½ × 3⅝ × 2⅝ loaf pan and bake at 350 degrees F. for 1 hour.

Yields 1 loaf

BUCKWHEAT CAKES

2	cups buckwheat flour		2½	cups scalded milk
2	cups all-purpose flour		½	cup (1 stick) butter, melted
1	tablespoon salt		2	tablespoons molasses
2	tablespoons sugar			
1	yeast cake dissolved in			
	2½ cups lukewarm water			

Combine the first six ingredients and allow to rise overnight. The next morning, add the butter, molasses, and just enough water for pouring consistency. Cook on a greased griddle as you would pancakes.

Yields 6 to 8 cakes

HOECAKES

It is said these cakes were so named because they were cooked over open fires on the flat side of a field hoe. This old recipe for hoecakes was provided by a former slave, Marrinda Jane Singleton. "Hoecakes was made of meal. You mix a cup of meal wid water an' pat it into small cakes. Grease it if got grease—dat keep it from stickin'. Den you rake out the ashes an' stick it on de hoe into de bottom of de fire and cover it up. Let it cook 'bout five minutes, den take it out, rub de ashes off an' pick out de splinters. Wash it off wid warm water an' eat it fo' it cools. Don't taste like nothin' if you let it get cold." *(The Negro in Virginia)*

3	tablespoons bacon drippings, divided		1	teaspoon salt
2	tablespoons all-purpose flour		½–¾	cup milk
2	cups stone-ground yellow cornmeal		½	teaspoon baking soda
			1	egg

In a medium mixing bowl, mix 1 tablespoon of the drippings with the remaining ingredients. Preheat a cast-iron skillet over medium heat. Add the remaining 2 tablespoons of bacon drippings to the skillet. Drop round cakes of the cornmeal mixture, approximately 1 to 1½ inches thick, into the skillet. Fry for 1 or 2 minutes or until golden on each side. Drain on paper towels and serve hot.

Yields 10 to 12 cakes

Upon Booker T. Washington's death, the torch was passed to the next generation. Hampton graduate Robert Russa Moton served as the president of Tuskegee University from 1915 until 1935. He continued as president emeritus until his death in 1940. The torch passed between these two men represented and brightly illuminated the pride in the self-reliance and achievement of a free people. However, it also reflected the proud heritage, traditions, and the accomplishments of those who preceded this first generation born in freedom.

While president of Tuskegee Institute, Dr. Moton developed a credo that in many ways reflected lessons learned at Hampton that contributed to his personal growth and pride in the accomplishment of his ancestors. In part the credo reads:

> I believe in my own people—in their
> native worth—in their attainments of
> character, accomplishment and service
> —and their ultimate high destiny in the progress of mankind.
>
> I believe in my fellow-men of all races—in
> their right to an equal chance to share in all the
> good of this world—and my obligation to respect
> to the full their person and their personality.
>
> I believe in freedom—in freedom to live one's
> life to the full—to serve wherever there is need
> to achieve the limit of divine endowment. . . .

In his memoir, *Finding a Way Out,* President Moton would write, "Tuskegee Institute, with many other Negro educational institutions, [has] persistently preserved and used the folk music of their people, in keeping with the spirit of its origin, thus not only elevating it in the estimation of coloured people, but causing others also to appreciate its value and beauty."

CONDIMENTS AND PRESERVES

"The farm is steadily improving in productiveness. . . . It has over two thousand fruit trees . . . peach, pear, cherry, plum, and quince—in thriving condition."

—from *Memories of Old Hampton*

Sterilizing Jars for Pickling and Preserving

Wash jars in hot sudsy water and then rinse in scalding water. Next, place the jars in a very large pot and cover with hot water. Bring the water to a boil, cover the pot with a lid, and allow the jars to boil for an additional 15 minutes.

Turn the burner off and permit the jars to stand in the hot water until boiling ceases. Just prior to filling the jars, invert them on a clean absorbent kitchen towel to drain dry. Jars should be filled while they are still hot. Lids should be sterilized for 5 minutes or according to manufacturer's directions.

Hampton lady preserving fruit and vegetables
(Courtesy of Hampton University Archives)

GREEN TOMATO CHOWCHOW

This is a delicious condiment with pork or beef, or serve it with greens or other vegetables. Chowchow is the salsa or mojo of the South!

1	peck green tomatoes, sliced	8	cups brown sugar
12	large white onions, sliced thin	2	tablespoons dry mustard
1	cup pickling salt	1	tablespoon table salt
3	quarts cider vinegar	20	small hot red peppers, sliced thin
10	thinly sliced green bell peppers	1½	tablespoons celery seeds
8	diced sweet red bell peppers	2½	tablespoons whole cloves
6	garlic cloves, minced	2½	tablespoons ground allspice
		2	3-inch cinnamon sticks
		3–4	bay leaves

Sprinkle the sliced tomatoes and onions with pickling salt. Refrigerate for 12 hours or overnight. Rinse in clear water and drain. Bring the vinegar to boil. Add the green peppers, red peppers, garlic, brown sugar, dry mustard, and table salt. Add the drained tomatoes, hot peppers, celery seeds, cloves, allspice, cinnamon sticks, and bay leaves. Reduce the heat and simmer for approximately 1 hour, or until the tomatoes are transparent. Stir frequently. When done, place in sterile, hot, airtight jars. Seal according to the manufacturer's directions.

Yields approximately 2 quarts

CREAMY FRESH BERRY BUTTER

Flavored butters are delicious with hot, fresh from the oven, homemade bread.

1	cup fresh berries (raspberries, blueberries, *or* strawberries)	1	tablespoon light corn syrup
		2	tablespoons cream cheese
		1	cup (2 sticks) butter

Purée the berries, and, if necessary, press them through a strainer to remove seeds and skin; add corn syrup to the purée mixture, and set aside. In a separate bowl, beat the cream cheese and butter until light and fluffy, approximately 1 or 2 minutes. Add the berry purée and corn syrup and beat at medium speed until well blended, approximately 1 minute. Cover and refrigerate. Allow to stand at room temperature for approximately 30 minutes prior to serving. Serve with warm biscuits or bread.

Yields approximately 1½ cups

RASPBERRY BUTTER

1 cup fresh raspberries	2 tablespoons powdered sugar
2 tablespoons water	2 teaspoons raspberry liqueur
1½ tablespoons sugar	
½ cup (1 stick) unsalted butter, at room temperature	

Boil the raspberries, water, and sugar over medium heat for about 5 minutes. Strain the mixture into a small bowl. Place the raspberry mixture, butter, powdered sugar, and raspberry liqueur into a blender or food processor. Blend until smooth. Transfer to a small serving container, cover, and chill for 1 hour prior to serving.

Yields approximately 1½ cups

Herb Butter

½   cup butter
2   tablespoons cream cheese
¼   cup fresh herbs (chives, thyme,
      rosemary, sage, marjoram)

¹⁄₁₆   teaspoon lemon juice

Combine the butter, cream cheese, herbs, and lemon juice, and process until smooth; shape and refrigerate. Serve with your favorite vegetables.

Yields approximately ¾ cup

Homemade Horseradish Sauce

2–4   horseradish roots, peeled and
        grated

½   cup white vinegar
½   teaspoon salt

Mix all ingredients well and pack into a clean jar. Seal tightly and refrigerate. May be served immediately or stored for up to 1 week. Delicious with lamb, roast beef, and other meats.

Yields ¾ to 1 cup

SOUR CREAM AND CHIVE HORSERADISH SAUCE

1	cup cultured sour cream	¼	teaspoon salt
½	teaspoon Dijon mustard	⅛	teaspoon paprika
2	tablespoons grated fresh horseradish	¼	cup chopped chives

In a small bowl, combine the above ingredients. Cover and refrigerate until ready for use. Great with cold meats or prime rib.

Yields approximately 1 cup

PORT WINE JELLY

2	cups port	⅛	teaspoon ground cloves
3	cups sugar	½	teaspoon grated orange rind
⅛	teaspoon ground cinnamon	½	cup liquid pectin
⅛	teaspoon ground allspice		

In the top of a double boiler, over rapidly boiling water, combine the above ingredients. Stirring constantly, cook for 2 minutes. Remove the boiler to the direct heat of a burner and cook over high heat until the mixture comes to a full rolling boil. Add the liquid pectin. Bring to another rolling boil and cook for an additional 1 minute, stirring constantly. Remove the pan from the heat, and skim the foam from the liquid. Ladle into sterile hot jars and process according to the manufacturer's directions.

Yields approximately 4 half-pint jars

Rachel kneading dough
(Courtesy of Hampton University Archives)

HERB VINEGAR

1	gallon white vinegar	1	sprig chervil
1	dozen peppercorns	1	sprig basil
3	sprigs rosemary	5	shallots, peeled and sliced
3	sprigs dried thyme		

Bottle the ingredients. Store in a cool dark place for 2 weeks, then strain through cheesecloth. Store in sterile bottles and cork tightly.

Yields 1 gallon

HOT PEPPER VINEGAR

A bottle of my grandfather's hot pepper vinegar could always be found on the Formica table in my grandparents' kitchen. There, suspended in amber vinegar, the pickled peppers waited to spice up the flavor of greens, or smothered cabbage. And the longer the mixture sat, the hotter the vinegar got!

2	dozen small hot chili peppers, both red and green	2	teaspoons sugar
1	large garlic clove, crushed	1¾	cups cider vinegar

Wash the peppers. Place them in a bowl with the crushed garlic. Bring the vinegar and sugar to a boil and pour over the peppers and garlic. Cover with a towel and allow to cool. Fill two sterilized pint jars with the mixture, seal, and let set for 2 weeks. Great served over greens.

Yields 2 pints

RASPBERRY VINEGAR

1	pint raspberries	2	tablespoons sugar
2	cups white wine vinegar	1	sprig fresh rosemary

Wash the berries, removing any stems or leaves. Place the berries in a nonreactive bowl and stir together with the vinegar and sugar. Cover the bowl with a clean tea towel and allow to stand at room temperature for 2 days. Carefully strain the liquid from the berries, discarding the pulp. Strain the liquid through a triple thickness of rinsed and squeezed cheesecloth. Transfer to a bottle with a tight-fitting lid; add the sprig of rosemary to the bottle before sealing. Excellent for dressing salad. Keeps indefinitely when stored in a cool, dark place.

Yields approximately 2 cups

BRANDIED PEACHES

½	pound brown sugar	1¼	teaspoons grated lemon rind
½	pound granulated sugar	⅛	teaspoon almond extract
1	tablespoon ground cinnamon	2	pounds small clingstone peaches
1	tablespoon lemon juice		Brandy

Combine the sugars and cinnamon; set aside. In a large kettle, combine the lemon juice, lemon rind, almond extract, and peaches together with sufficient water to cover the peaches. Bring the peaches to a simmer and continue to simmer until just tender. Take care not to boil. Drain the peaches and remove their skins. Place 1 inch of the sugar mixture on the bottom of two quart jars. Arrange one or two peaches on top of the sugar mixture. Alternate layers of peaches and sugar until the jar is filled. Add enough brandy to cover completely and screw lid on tightly. Store in a dark place for 2 to 3 months before serving. Great served warm over Peach Brandy Pound Cake (page 219).

10 to 12 servings

SPICED PEACHES

2	cups water		2	Bay leaves
3½	cups dark brown sugar		7	pounds medium-size peaches, peeled and pitted
3	cups apple cider vinegar		2½	cups sugar
1	tablespoon whole cloves			Juice of ½ lemon
1	tablespoon whole allspice		2	Bay leaves
2	cinnamon sticks			
2	1-inch pieces gingerroot			

In a medium pot, combine the water, dark brown sugar, and vinegar. Bring to a boil. Place the spices and two bay leaves in a spice bag and add to the liquid in the pot. Bring to a second boil. Cook the peaches a few at a time until barely tender, approximately 5 minutes. With a slotted spoon, remove each batch to a bag. When the last batch has been removed, add 2 cups of the remaining sugar and bring to a rapid boil. Pour the syrup over the peaches, cover, and let stand overnight. Reheat the peaches and syrup, then pack the fruit into quart jars. Add the remaining ½ cup of sugar and lemon juice to the syrup, bring to a boil, and pour over the peaches. Leave ½ inch of space at the top of the jar. Add one bay leaf to each jar. Screw the lids in place. Place in a hot-water bath and process for 20 minutes or according to the manufacturer's directions. Excellent with roast pork.

Yields approximately 2 quarts

PICKLED PEACHES

8	pounds (approximately 24) firm ripe peaches		6	cups granulated sugar
	Whole cloves		2	cups light brown sugar
			2	cups cider vinegar

Wash the peaches but do not peel them. Remove the buds from the clove stems and insert two stems in each peach. In a large bowl, combine the sugars and peaches; mix well, cover, and allow to stand overnight. Transfer the juice that has accumulated in the bowl to a kettle and boil over high heat, stirring constantly, until the syrup has thickened slightly. Stir the vinegar into the thickened syrup, add the peaches, stir, and simmer over medium-low heat until the peaches are just fork-tender and slightly translucent. Transfer the peaches to four sterilized jars (see the procedure on page 193). Ladle the syrup over the peaches; wipe the rims of the jars with a clean damp cloth. Seal with lids according to the manufacturer's directions and place them in a canner or on a rack set in a deep kettle, adding enough warm water to cover by 2 inches. Bring the water to a boil and process, covered, for 10 minutes. Transfer the jars with canning tongs to a folded kitchen towel and allow to cool before storing in a cool dark place.

Yields approximately 4 quarts

Brandied Pears

½	cup sugar		2	cups brandy
1½	tablespoons lemon juice		2	cups water
1½	tablespoons grated lemon zest		2–3	pounds perfect pears, peeled, halved,
1	3-inch cinnamon stick			and cored
½	teaspoon whole allspice			
	berries (about 5 to 7)			

In a large pot, combine the sugar, lemon juice and zest, cinnamon stick, allspice, brandy, and water. Bring to a boil; add the pears, a few at a time; and cook until tender, approximately 20 to 30 minutes. Discard the cinnamon stick and pack the pears into hot sterilized jars. Leave ½ inch headroom. Adjust the lids, and process in a hot-water bath 20 minutes for pint jars, 25 minutes for quart jars.

Yields 1 quart

VERY SPICY SPICED PEARS

8	pounds Seckel or Kieffer pears		1-inch piece fresh gingerroot
8	pounds sugar	2	tablespoons whole cloves
2	cups boiling water	2	tablespoons whole allspice
2	cups white vinegar	8	3-inch cinnamon sticks
½	lemon rind	8	small bay leaves

Wash the pears and set them aside to drain. In a large pot, combine the sugar, water, vinegar, lemon rind, ginger, cloves, and allspice. Bring to a quick boil; reduce the heat, and simmer for 30 minutes. While the mixture is simmering, peel the pears. Add the pears to the simmering sugar mixture and simmer for an additional 30 minutes. Remove the ginger. Divide the pears and cinnamon sticks among eight pint jars. Slide one bay leaf to the side of each jar. Ladle boiling liquid and ½ tablespoon of the spices contained in the liquid over the pears. Leave ½ inch headroom. Process in a hot-water bath for 20 minutes. Excellent with pork dishes or served cold or warm as dessert or with poundcake.

Yields 8 pints

PEAR HONEY

8	cups peeled, cored, and coarsely chopped ripe pears		Rind of a lemon, cut into pieces
5¼	cups sugar	¾	cup crushed pineapple with juice
	Juice of a lemon	1	3-inch cinnamon stick

In a large, heavy pot, combine all ingredients; slowly bring to a boil, and then simmer for 45 to 60 minutes or until pears are transparent. Stir frequently to prevent scorching. Remove the cinnamon stick and pour the boiling mixture into hot sterilized jars, allowing ½ inch headroom. Process in a hot-water bath for 20 minutes. Great with hot biscuits or plain.

Yields 7 pints

VIOLET HONEY

Sweet-scented, heart-shaped violet flowers impart a delicate flavor to honey. Just be sure that the petals are washed clean and have not been sprayed with pesticides.

2   cups clear honey
2   cup fresh violet petals

Heat the honey until it becomes liquid and pours easily. Add the violet petals. Allow to cool to luke-warm. Pour into a glass container and seal. Let rest undisturbed for approximately ten days. Reheat, strain, and discard the violets. Return the honey to the bottle and reseal.

Yields 2 cups

VANILLA EXTRACT

You need never run out of vanilla extract again. All you need is a 1-liter bottle of rum and three vanilla beans. Place the beans in the bottle with the rum and set it aside in a cool, dark place for 30 days. The vanilla can be used in recipes at this time, but the longer it sets, the stronger it gets. Replace what you use with more liquor. When the contents begin to taste only weakly of vanilla, start over with a new bottle of rum and new vanilla beans.

PICKLED WATERMELON RIND

1 pound watermelon, green
  outer rind and pink flesh
  removed
¾ cup salt
3¾ quarts water
3 trays ice cubes
9 cups sugar
3 cups white vinegar

1¼ tablespoons whole cloves
1 tablespoon whole allspice
4 1-inch pieces gingerroot
2 star anise
3 cups water
1 lemon, sliced thin
10 4-inch cinnamon sticks

Cut the rind into 1-inch squares (approximately 12 cups). Dissolve the salt in the water and add the ice cubes. Pour this iced water over the watermelon cubes and allow to stand for 5 to 7 hours. Drain the water from the rind and rinse in cold water. Place the rind in a medium pot, cover with cold water, and cook until fork-tender, about 10 minutes. Drain and set aside. In a medium saucepan, combine the sugar, vinegar, spices, ginger, star anise, and 3 cups of water. Bring to a rapid boil, reduce the heat, and simmer for 10 minutes. Add the rind, lemon slices, and additional water to cover, if required. Boil very gently—almost a simmer—until the melon cubes are transparent and tender, approximately 10 minutes. Pack into hot sterilized pint jars with one cinnamon stick per jar. Cover with boiling syrup. Leave ½ inch headroom. Process in a boiling-water bath for 10 minutes, or follow the manufacturer's directions.

Yields 10 pints

APPLE BUTTER

8 pounds ripe apples
  (Jonathan, Winesap, or
  other flavorful apple)
4 cups sweet cider
3 cups firmly packed dark
  brown sugar

1 teaspoon ground cloves
2¼ teaspoons ground cinnamon
¼ teaspoon ground allspice
  Zest of 1 lemon

Wash the apples. Remove their stems, core them, and quarter them. In a large pot, over medium heat, cook the apples in the cider until they are soft. Remove the pot from the heat and allow to cool before processing the apples into a purée. To each cup of purée, add ½ cup sugar at a time, up to 3 cups, depending on taste. Add the spices and lemon zest. Return the fruit to the pot and continue to cook over low heat, stirring constantly, until the sugar is dissolved and the mixture thickens. Test doneness by placing a small amount of the mixture on a cold saucer. The outside surface of the portion tested should show a slight sheen upon standing. When no rim of liquid separates from around the edge of the butter, it is done. Pour into sterilized jars and seal according to the manufacturer's directions.

Yields 3 to 4 pints

DAMSON PLUM BUTTER

Damson plums
Sugar

Wash, pit, and quarter the plums. Place them in a large saucepan with just enough water to prevent burning. Cover and cook over medium heat until just softened, approximately 10 to 15 minutes. Allow to cool slightly and then purée in a blender or process through a sieve. Add 1 cup of sugar for each cup of puree. Place the mixture in a heavy saucepan and cook over low heat for 1 to 1½ hours or until the plum butter is dark and thick. Pour immediately into hot sterilized jars and process: 10 minutes per pint—15 minutes per quart. Serve with hot biscuits.

One pound of plums will yield approximately 2 to 3 pints

Basketry—Zona Swayney
(Courtesy of Hampton University Archives)

Trip to the shore
(Courtesy of Hampton University Archives)

"When the delicious moonlight nights of early summer came on, the long veranda of the Barracks proved a most attractive promenade, and on Saturday and Sunday nights we girls would pace in couples back and forth and up and down, singing. . . . Or when tired of exercise, we would take our seats on the steps or on Grigg's Hall piazza and alternately sing ourselves and listen to the boys' voices as they sang in turn from their quarters in the Academic. And then sometimes there would float back to us from the creek the song of the berry-pickers returning from their day's work out at Sewell's Point. The song that they sang will always be associated in my mind with those glorious summer nights. . . ."

—From *Memories of Old Hampton*

MIXED FRUIT CONSERVE

4   pounds firm ripe peaches
1   pound medium firm ripe
      apricots
1   pound firm ripe cherries,
      washed, halved, and pitted
    Grated rind and juice of
      3 lemons

    Grated rind and juice of 2 oranges
6   cups sugar
2   cups seedless raisins
1½ cups chopped walnuts
1   cup brandy

Place the peaches and apricots into sufficient boiling water to cover them completely. Allow to boil rapidly for 2 to 3 minutes before transferring the fruit to a colander to drain and cool. When the fruit is sufficiently cool to handle, peel with a small paring knife, remove the pits, and chop it coarsely. Place the fruit in a 6- to 8-quart enamel or stainless-steel pot. Add the cherries and grated rinds and citrus juices. Stir in the sugar, cover the pot tightly, and allow to stand at room temperature overnight or for at least 12 hours. Over high heat, bring the mixture to a boil while stirring constantly with a wooden spoon. Take extreme care that the mixture does not scorch. Reduce the heat to low and simmer for 1 to 1½ hours. The fruit should be translucent and the mixture thick enough to hold its shape in a spoon. As the fruit begins to thicken, periodically stir up from the bottom of the pot to prevent scorching. Add the raisins, stir frequently, and cook for 15 minutes. Stir in the walnuts and brandy, mixing well. Pack in hot sterile jars and seal according to manufacturer's directions. Serve as an accompaniment to game and roast meats. Also delicious over ice cream.

Yields 6 to 8 pints

BLACKBERRY OR RASPBERRY JAM

Late summer is the time to "put up" your vegetables, preserves, and jams . . . then when served on winter mornings, you can again savor the flavor of summer.

The apples called for in this recipe take the place of the pectin used in many jam and jelly recipes.

½ cup crushed berries	3¾ cups sugar
3½ cups whole berries	2 Granny Smith apples, cored and cut
1 tablespoon fresh lemon juice	into small pieces

Combine all the ingredients in a medium pot. Cook over low heat until the mixture thickens—stirring frequently, from the bottom, to prevent sticking and scorching. Test for doneness by dropping a small amount on a plate. When done, it will hold its shape and stay in place. Pack in sterilized jars and seal according to the manufacturer's directions.

Yields 6 half-pint jars

PEACH JAM

3 pounds peaches	1¾ ounces powdered pectin
¾ cup lemon juice	5¼ cups sugar
1½ cinnamon sticks	

Wash, peel, pit, and crush the peaches. In a heavy pot, mix the crushed peaches and their juice with the lemon juice, cinnamon, and pectin. Bring to a boil. Add the sugar and bring to a second boil. Immediately remove from the heat. Skim the foam from the top of the jam. Pour the jam into sterile hot canning jars and process for 10 minutes in a boiling-water bath. Seal according to the manufacturer's directions.

Yields 6 half-pint jars

ROSE HIP JAM

Collect *unsprayed* rose hips after the first frost.

1 pound rose hips	Sugar
1 cup water	

In a heavy stainless-steel pan, simmer the rose hips in water until tender. Rub the hips through a fine sieve. Reweigh the pulp and allow ¼ pound of sugar for each ¼ pound of pulp. Simmer until thick. Place in hot sterile jars. Process according to the manufacturer's directions.

Yields 2 half-pint jars

CHERRY PRESERVES

Cherries
Sugar

Wash, stem, and remove pits from cherries. Weigh the cherries and measure an equal amount of sugar. If the cherries are very sweet, use only ¾ pound of sugar for every pound of fruit. In a large nonreactive container, alternate layers of sugar and cherries, with sugar being the first and last layer. Cover and allow to stand overnight. Transfer the mixture to a large stainless-steel pot and slowly bring to a boil. Stir frequently and simmer until the cherries are tender. Add a few drops of red food coloring if preserves are pale. With a slotted spoon, remove the cherries to hot sterile jars. Simmer the juice until it thickens, then pour over the fruit. Seal according to the manufacturer's directions and store in a cool place.

Yields 2 half-pint jars for each pound of cherries

PEACH PRESERVES

4	pounds fresh peaches	1-inch cinnamon stick	
7	cups sugar	Juice of 1 lemon	
3½	cups water		

Peel and quarter the peaches. Discard the pits. In a large pot, combine the sugar and water. Boil until the sugar is dissolved. Add the peaches and cinnamon stick, then cook for 10 minutes over moderate heat until the syrup clears and thickens, and the peaches are tender. Cover and allow to stand overnight, undisturbed. Discard the cinnamon stick. Remove the fruit to hot sterilized pint canning jars. Boil the remaining syrup with the lemon juice, stirring frequently, until the syrup thickens to the consistency of honey. Distribute equally over fruit in canning jars. Allow ½ inch headroom. Process in a hot-water bath for 10 minutes.

Yields 4 pints

STRAWBERRY PRESERVES

2	quarts firm tart strawberries	Juice of 1 lemon	
8	cups sugar	4½	cups sugar

Remove the stems and leaves from the strawberries. Wash the berries and set aside. In a large bowl, alternate layers of sugar and strawberries. Refrigerate for 10 to 12 hours to draw out the juice. Place the berries in a large pot and, over medium-high heat, bring the mixture to a quick boil. Stir gently so as not to break the berries. Continue to boil, stirring frequently to prevent scorching, until the liquid reaches a temperature of 10 to 12 degrees F. above boiling (222–224 degrees F. at sea level). Add the lemon juice and sugar and cook for an additional 3 minutes. Cover and allow berries to stand undisturbed for 24 hours. Bring to a boil before ladling into hot sterile ½-pint canning jars. Process according to the manufacturer's directions, or in a boiling-water bath for 10 minutes.

Yields 3 pints

BREAD-AND-BUTTER PICKLES

1¼	gallons small cucumbers, unpared	4	cups cider vinegar
3½	cups small white pearl onions	4	cups brown sugar
1	green bell pepper, seeds and membranes removed, chopped coarse	2	teaspoons whole allspice
		2¼	tablespoons mustard seeds
		1	tablespoon whole cloves
1	red bell pepper, seeds and membranes removed, chopped coarse	¼	teaspoon ground turmeric
		½	teaspoon celery seeds
½	cup pickling salt	¾	teaspoon ground ginger
			1-inch cinnamon stick

Cut the unpared cucumbers into ½-inch slices. Place them in a nonreactive bowl together with onions and peppers. Cover with the pickling salt and a weighted lid. Refrigerate for 12 hours. Drain and thoroughly rinse in cold, running water. Place in a nonreactive colander to drain and set aside.

In a medium kettle, combine the vinegar, brown sugar, and spices. Bring to a quick boil over high heat. Reduce the heat to medium high and gradually add the vegetables. Do not allow the mixture to boil. Pour the mixture into hot sterile jars. Seal and process according to the manufacturer's directions.

Yields 6 to 8 pints

SOUR PICKLES

3	tablespoons mixed whole pickling spice	2¼	cups salt
3	tablespoons pickling dill	2	cups white vinegar
40	small pickling cucumbers (3 to 5 inches long), well scrubbed	3	gallons hot water
			Peppercorns
		11	garlic cloves
			Bay leaves

In a large stone crock, place half the pickling spice, then cover with half of the dill. Add the cucumbers. Place the remaining pickling spice and dill on top of the cucumbers. In a large stainless-steel pot, combine 1½ cups of the salt with the 2 cups of vinegar and 2 gallons of the hot water. Cool this brine and pour it over the cucumbers. Cover with a weighted plate to hold the pickles at least 2 inches below the brine. Allow to pickle at room temperature for 3 to 4 weeks, removing scum from the surface daily. When the pickles are an even color without any white spots, they are ready to pack. Pierce through both ends of each pickle with a sterilized knitting needle or ice pick. Divide among nine hot sterilized quart jars. Place five peppercorns, a garlic clove, and a bay leaf in each jar. In a large pot, bring 1 gallon of water, ¾ cup salt, 1 cup white vinegar, and the 2 remaining garlic cloves to a boil. Pour over the pickles. Seal according to the manufacturer's directions or process in a hot-water bath for 15 minutes.

Yields 9 quarts

DESSERTS

"Uncle Bailey, what was the most eventful day of your life? 'The day the stars fell. I was eight years old but I remember it as well as if it was yesterday. They began to fall about sundown and fell all night. They fell like rain. They looked like little balls about as big as marbles with a long streak of fire to them. . . . A few days later it began to snow and snowed three days and nights.'"

—Bailey Cunningham, from *Weevils in the Wheat*

SOUTHERN BUTTERMILK POUND CAKE

1	cup (2 sticks) butter, softened		⅛	teaspoon ground allspice
2½	cups sugar		½	teaspoon baking soda
4	eggs, at room temperature		2	teaspoons hot water
3	cups sifted all-purpose flour			

Preheat the oven to 350 degrees F. Grease and flour a 10-inch tube pan and set aside. Cream the butter and sugar. Add the eggs one at a time, beating well after each addition. Stir in the flour and allspice. Dissolve the baking soda in the hot water and add to the flour mixture. Mix well, pour the batter into the pan, and bake for 1 hour.

10 to 12 servings

SOUR CREAM POUND CAKE

1	cup (2 sticks) butter, softened		3	cups cake flour, sifted
2½	cups sugar		1	tablespoon baking powder
6	eggs, at room temperature		1	tablespoon vanilla extract
1	cup cultured sour cream			

Preheat the oven to 325 degrees F. Grease and flour a 12-cup bundt or tube pan and set aside. In a large bowl, cream the butter with an electric mixer. Gradually add the sugar and continue beating until light and fluffy. Add the eggs, one at a time, beating well after each addition. Add the sour cream and mix thoroughly.

In a separate bowl, sift together the cake flour and baking powder. Add the flour mixture to the butter mixture, and beat in the vanilla extract for 2 minutes. Pour into the prepared pan and bake for 1 hour. Serve with a dollop of whipped cream and a Brandied Peach half (see page 200).

10 to 12 servings

MY GRANDMOTHER'S POUND CAKE WITH PEACHES AND CREAM

My mouth waters at the thought of my grandmother's warm pound cake topped with cool peaches in syrup and ice cream.

1 pound butter	3 cups all-purpose flour
2 cups sugar	1 cup evaporated milk
1 teaspoon vanilla extract	Brown Sugar Bourbon Peaches
6 eggs	(below)
1 tablespoon baking powder	

Preheat the oven to 325 degrees F. Grease and flour a tube or bundt pan and set aside. Cream together the butter, sugar, vanilla, and eggs. In a separate bowl, sift together the baking powder and flour. Add the flour mixture to butter mixture, 1 cup at a time. Add the evaporated milk and beat well. Pour the batter into the prepared pan and bake for approximately 1 hour. Serve with Brown Sugar Bourbon Peaches and vanilla ice cream.

BROWN SUGAR BOURBON PEACHES WITH VANILLA ICE CREAM

¾ cup bourbon	2 tablespoons fresh lemon juice
½ cup firmly packed dark brown sugar	1 tablespoon vanilla extract
¼ cup (½ stick) butter	4 peaches, peeled, pitted, and sliced
½ teaspoon ground cinnamon	Vanilla ice cream

Combine the bourbon and next five ingredients in a heavy medium skillet over medium-low heat. Stir until the sugar dissolves. Add the peaches and stir until heated through. Place a slice of pound cake in a bowl. Place a scoop of ice cream on top of the cake. Top with peaches and sauce and serve.

10 to 12 servings

PEACH BRANDY POUND CAKE

3½	cups granulated sugar		½	teaspoon salt
½	cup dark brown sugar		1	cup sour cream
1	cup (2 sticks) butter, softened		1¼	teaspoons orange extract
6	eggs		2	teaspoons vanilla extract
3	cups all-purpose flour		¼	teaspoon ground allspice
¼	teaspoon baking soda		½	teaspoon lemon zest
2½	teaspoons baking powder		½	cup peach brandy, divided

Preheat the oven to 325 degrees F. Cream together the sugars and butter until light and fluffy. Add the eggs, one at a time, mixing after each addition, until all the eggs have been used. Set aside.

In a separate bowl, sift together the flour, baking soda, baking powder, and salt, and set aside. In another separate bowl, combine the sour cream, extracts, allspice, lemon zest, and 3 tablespoons of the brandy. Beginning and ending with the flour, combine the flour mixture, alternating, with the sour cream and butter mixtures. Mix until just blended; then pour into a tube pan or a 12-cup bundt pan. Bake for 1 to 1¼ hours. Cool on a rack for 25 minutes prior to serving. Drizzle the remaining brandy over the cake while it's still warm.

10 to 12 servings

COCONUT CAKE

1	cup (2 sticks) butter		1	teaspoon baking soda
2	cups sugar		1	cup buttermilk
5	eggs, separated		1	tablespoon vanilla extract
2¼	cups all-purpose, presifted flour		1	cup sweetened coconut

Preheat the oven to 350 degrees F. Grease and flour two 9-inch round cake pans and set aside. In a large mixing bowl, cream together the butter and sugar. Add the egg yolks, one at a time. Beat well. Add the flour and baking soda alternately with the buttermilk, vanilla, and coconut. With a clean beater, beat the egg whites until peaks form but are not stiff. Gently, fold the beaten egg whites into the batter and pour into the prepared pans. Bake for 35 to 40 minutes.

8 to 10 servings

FROSTING

1 12-ounce package cream cheese	1-pound box powdered sugar
½ cup (1 stick) butter	2 teaspoons vanilla extract
	1 cup chopped walnuts

Cream together the cream cheese, butter, and sugar. Add the vanilla and mix well. Frost each layer. After stacking the layers, smooth the frosting over the top and sides of the cake. Garnish the top with chopped walnuts.

WHITE FRUIT CAKE

A fruit cake's flavor is enhanced with age. Age for at least 30 days before serving by storing in a cool dry place. Once a week or so, slightly moisten with equal parts brandy and Grand Marnier.

1 pound candied cherries	2 teaspoons fresh lemon juice
1 pound candied pineapple	2 teaspoons ground nutmeg
½ pound citron	12 beaten egg whites
1 cup white seedless raisins	4 cups sifted all-purpose flour
½ cup brandy	2 teaspoons baking powder
½ pound blanched almonds	1½ cup pecans
¼ cup rose water	1½ cups walnuts
1 pound butter	Zest of 1 orange
2 cups sugar	

Prepare the fruit by slicing the cherries in half, if necessary, and soaking all of the fruit in brandy for 72 hours. Soak the blanched almonds in rose water overnight. Prepare aluminum tube pans by lining the bottom with greased brown paper cut to fit. Preheat the oven to 275 degrees F. Cream together the butter and sugar. Add the lemon juice, nutmeg, and egg whites. Sift together the flour and baking soda, saving enough to dust the fruits and nuts. (Dusting prevents them from sticking together.) Mix the flour and butter mixtures well. Add the flour-dusted fruits and nuts to the batter and stir to combine. Bake for 3 to 3½ hours. Keep a pan of water in the oven to maintain moisture while baking.

10 to 12 servings

RED BOURBON PECAN CAKE

1½ cups sifted all-purpose flour, divided	1½ teaspoons baking soda
1 cup chopped pecans	1 teaspoon ground nutmeg
1 cup seedless raisins	½ teaspoon ground allspice
½ cup (1 stick) softened butter	½ teaspoon ground cinnamon
½ cup light brown sugar	Scant dash of salt
1 cup plus 2 tablespoons granulated sugar	1 teaspoon orange zest
3 eggs, separated	½ cup bourbon
	Pecans
	Maraschino cherries

Preheat the oven to 325 degrees F. Line the bottom of a greased 10-inch tube pan with greased brown paper. Mix ½ cup of the flour with the pecans and raisins, coating thoroughly.

In a separate bowl, cream the butter, gradually add the sugar, and continue to cream until light and fluffy. Add the egg yolks, one at a time, beating well after each addition. In a separate bowl, combine the remaining flour with baking soda, spices, and salt. Add the flour mixture to the butter mixture ⅓ cup at a time, mixing well after each addition. Add the orange zest and floured nuts and raisins, mixing well. Add the bourbon, mixing well. Beat the egg whites until very stiff and fold in. Fold the batter into the prepared pan and press down firmly; allow to set for 10 minutes. Decorate the top with pecan halves and maraschino cherries. Bake for 1 hour to 1 hour and 20 minutes or until a wooden tester inserted in its center comes out clean. Cool for 1 or 2 hours and then turn out.

8 to 10 servings

BLACK WALNUT CAKE

1 cup (2 sticks) butter, at room temperature	3 cups all-purpose flour
½ cup solid shortening	¼ teaspoon salt
3 cups sugar	1 teaspoon baking powder
5 eggs	1 teaspoon vanilla extract
1 cup half-and-half	1 cup black walnuts, coarsely chopped
⅔ cup whole milk	1 teaspoon black walnut extract

Preheat the oven to 350 degrees F. Butter and flour three 9-inch baking pans. Cream together the butter, shortening, and sugar. Add the eggs one at a time, mixing well after each addition. In a separate bowl, add the half-and-half to the milk and set aside. Next, combine the flour, salt, and baking powder; sift this into the butter mixture, alternating with the milk mixture. Add the vanilla extract, black walnuts, and black walnut extract; mix well. Pour the batter into the prepared pans and bake for 1 hour.

FROSTING

2 pounds powdered sugar	⅓ cup half-and-half
1 cup (2 sticks) butter, softened	1½ cups finely chopped black walnuts
1 teaspoon vanilla extract	

Cream together the sugar, butter, and vanilla extract; mix well. Gradually add the half-and-half until a smooth consistency is reached. Smooth onto each layer. After stacking the layers, smooth the frosting over the top and sides of the cake. Garnish the top and sides with chopped walnuts.

8 to 10 servings

BLACKBERRY JAM CAKE

3 cups sifted all-purpose flour	¼ cup brown sugar
1 teaspoon baking soda	1 cup granulated sugar
1 tablespoon ground cinnamon	4 eggs, separated
2 teaspoons ground cloves	1 cup buttermilk
1 tablespoon ground allspice	2 teaspoons vanilla extract
1 cup (2 sticks) butter, softened	1 cup seedless blackberry jam

Preheat the oven to 325 degrees F. Grease and flour two 9-inch round cake pans and set aside. Sift together the flour, baking soda, and spices, and set aside. Cream the butter, gradually adding the sugars; continue to cream until light and fluffy. Add the yolks, one at a time, beating well after each addition. Add the flour mixture alternating with buttermilk. Beat until smooth. Next, add the vanilla extract and jam. Mix well. In a separate bowl, beat the egg whites until stiff peaks form, and fold into the batter. Pour batter into prepared baking pans. Bake for 30 minutes. Increase the heat to 350 degrees and bake for an additional 50 to 60 minutes or until a tester inserted in the center comes out clean. Cool and remove from the pans.

FROSTING

1 12-ounce package cream cheese	1 pound powdered sugar
½ cup (1 stick) butter	2 teaspoons vanilla extract
	2 pints fresh blackberries

Cream together the cream cheese, butter, and sugar. Add the vanilla and mix well. Frost each layer. After stacking the layers, smooth the frosting over the top and sides of the cake. Fill the center of the cake with fresh berries, and garnish its base with a cluster of berries.

8 to 10 servings

RED VELVET CAKE

½   cup (1 stick) butter
1½ cups sugar
2   eggs
1   teaspoon vanilla extract
1½ ounces red food coloring
2   level tablespoons cocoa

1   teaspoon baking soda
1   teaspoon baking powder
1   teaspoon vinegar
1   cup buttermilk
2½ cups cake flour
1   teaspoon salt

Preheat the oven to 350 degrees F. Grease and flour two 9-inch layer pans. Cream together the butter and sugar. Add the eggs, beating after each addition. Add the remaining ingredients, mixing well. Pour into the prepared baking pans and bake for 30 to 35 minutes until golden or until a tester inserted in the center comes out clean. Cool and remove from the pan.

FROSTING

6   tablespoons flour
1   cup granulated sugar
1   cup water

1   cup (2 sticks) butter
1   teaspoon vanilla extract

Mix together the flour, sugar, and water, bring to a boil, and cook until slightly clear. Cool for 2 hours. Cream the butter and add to the cooled flour mixture. Add vanilla extract and beat until light and fluffy.

Yields enough to frost 1 cake

RASPBERRY AND SHERRY CUSTARD

4	cups half-and-half	1	egg
¾	cup sugar	1	teaspoon rum flavoring
3	tablespoons cornstarch	½	cup cream sherry
⅛	teaspoon salt	2	tablespoons raspberry jam
3	egg yolks		

In a heavy saucepan, combine the half-and-half, sugar, cornstarch, and salt. Bring to a quick boil over high heat, stirring constantly. Immediately reduce the heat to medium high and continue to boil until the mixture is slightly thickened. Beat together the egg yolks and whole egg. Add 1 cup of the hot cream mixture to the beaten egg mixture, stir, and return to the hot cream mixture. Continue cooking, stirring constantly, until the custard is thick. Do not let it boil. Add the rum flavoring, sherry, and jam. Stir and cool. Top your favorite pound cake with fresh raspberries and pour custard over the cake and raspberries. Top with dollops of whipped cream.

Yields approximately 5 cups

CARROT CAKE

2	cups sugar	1⅓	cups salad oil
3	cups flour	2	eggs, beaten
1	teaspoon baking powder	1	cup chopped pecans
1	tablespoon baking soda	1	cup crushed pineapple, drained
½	teaspoon salt	1	teaspoon vanilla extract
1	teaspoon ground cinnamon	1	teaspoon lemon extract
2	cups coarsely grated carrots		

Preheat the oven to 350 degrees F. Grease and flour two large loaf pans or one bundt pan. Measure the sugar into a mixing bowl and sift the remaining dry ingredients into the bowl. Add the carrots, salad oil, and eggs. Beat until well mixed. Add the remaining ingredients and stir. Pour the batter into the prepared pan(s). Place in the preheated oven and bake for approximately 1 hour or until a toothpick inserted in the middle comes out clean. Remove the cake(s) from the oven and allow to cool. When completely cool, frost with Cream Cheese Glaze (below).

10 to 12 servings

CREAM CHEESE GLAZE

¼   cup (½ stick) butter
4-ounce package cream
    cheese, softened

2   cups powdered sugar
½   cup pineapple juice

Cream the butter and cheese together. Add the powdered sugar and blend until smooth. Then slowly add pineapple juice until the mixture is just thin enough to drizzle over the cake without being runny.

CHOCOLATE-COVERED STRAWBERRIES

2   dozen large strawberries
12 ounces semisweet chocolate

¼   teaspoon almond extract

Wash the strawberries and set them aside. Do not destem. Melt the chocolate over a double boiler, stirring frequently; when it's satiny smooth, remove it from the heat and stir in the extract. Dip one strawberry at a time half to three-quarters of the way into chocolate, then place it on a waxed-paper-covered cookie sheet. Refrigerate until the chocolate sets. I bet you can't eat just one. Delicious served with champagne.

24 strawberries

BUTTERMILK PECAN PIE

½   cup (1 stick) butter
2   cups sugar
5   eggs
2   tablespoons all-purpose flour
2   tablespoons lemon extract

1   tablespoon vanilla extract
1   cup buttermilk
1¼ cups chopped pecans
1   unbaked pie shell

Preheat the oven to 350 degrees F. In a medium mixing bowl, cream the butter and sugar together, mixing well. Add the eggs, one at a time, beating well after each addition. Add the remaining ingredients and stir well. Pour into the pie shell and bake for 55 minutes or until set in the middle. Test doneness by inserting a knife into the middle; the knife should come out clean. Cool on a wire rack and store in the refrigerator.

8 servings

PECAN PIE

3   eggs
¾   cup granulated sugar
1   cup dark corn syrup
1   teaspoon vanilla extract

¼   cup melted butter
1   cup pecans
1   unbaked pie shell

Beat the eggs and sugar together. Stir in the syrup, vanilla, and butter. Place the pecans on the bottom of the pie shell and cover with syrup. The pecans will rise during baking. Bake at 350 degrees F. for 40 to 45 minutes or until done.

6 to 8 servings

BLACK WALNUT PIE

¼ cup (½ stick) butter
½ cup light brown sugar
½ cup granulated sugar
1 teaspoon ground cinnamon
⅛ teaspoon ground allspice
2 teaspoons vanilla extract
1 cup dark corn syrup

3 eggs, well beaten
2 tablespoons boiling water
¼ cup black walnut meats, coarsely crushed
1 unbaked 9-inch pie shell
Whipped cream or black walnut ice cream

Preheat the oven to 350 degrees F. In a medium saucepan, melt the butter and add the sugars, spices, vanilla, and corn syrup. Stir to dissolve. Add the eggs and stir in the water. Place the walnuts in the pie shell and pour the mixture over them. Bake for 50 minutes. Let the pie cool and serve with the whipped cream or ice cream.

6 to 8 servings

LEMON MERINGUE PIE

1¼ cups all-purpose flour
1¼ teaspoons sugar
¾ teaspoon salt
2½ tablespoons chilled, unsalted butter, cut into pieces

¼ cup chilled solid shortening
9 tablespoons ice water

In a medium bowl, sift together the flour, sugar, and salt. Cut in the butter and shortening until the mixture resembles coarse meal. Stir in the water just until the mixture comes together. Form the dough into a ball and then into a thin disk. Wrap in plastic and chill for at least 30 minutes.

FILLING

1¼ cups sugar	4 large egg yolks (reserve whites)
¼ cup cornstarch	½ cup fresh lemon juice
3 tablespoons all-purpose flour	2 tablespoons (¼ stick) unsalted butter
¼ teaspoon salt	1½ tablespoons grated lemon peel
1½ cups cold water	

In a heavy, medium saucepan, combine the sugar, cornstarch, flour, and salt. Gradually whisk in the water. Boil over medium heat for 1 minute while stirring constantly. In a separate bowl, whisk the egg yolks. Gradually whisk in some of the hot cornstarch mixture. Return the mixture to the saucepan and boil until very thick, again stirring constantly, about 5 minutes; remove from the heat and whisk in the juice, butter, and lemon peel. Cool completely and then spoon the mixture into the crust; cover, chill, and make the meringue. If the mixture is not completely cooled, your pie will be weepy and the crust will become soggy.

MERINGUE

4	egg whites
¼	cup sugar

Preheat the oven to 350 degrees F. With a wire whisk or electric beater, beat the egg whites to a froth. Add the sugar and continue beating until the meringue is sufficiently stiff to stand in firm peaks on the beaters when they are lifted from the bowl. Spread the meringue on top of the cooled custard, mounding it slightly in the center. Create decorative swirls with a spatula. Bake in the upper third of the oven for about 15 minutes or until the meringue is firm and delicately browned.

6 to 8 servings

KEY LIME PIE

1   9-inch pie shell, prebaked

FILLING

5 eggs, separated	¾ cup fresh lime juice
14 ounces sweetened condensed milk	1 cup heavy cream, whipped, for garnish

Preheat the oven to 325 degrees F. Either whisk or beat the eggs for 5 minutes until thick. Slowly add the condensed milk and lime juice; mix well and then set aside. In a separate bowl, beat the egg whites until soft peaks form. Do not beat them stiff. Gently fold the egg yolk and egg white mixtures together. Spoon at once into a cool pie shell. Bake for 20 minutes or until the filling is firm. Serve at room temperature with a dollop of whipped cream.

6 to 8 servings

CHERRY PIE

1 tablespoon flour	¹⁄₁₆ teaspoon lemon extract
½ cup light brown sugar	2 cups fresh cherries, pitted
1 cup granulated sugar	1 9-inch pie shell, prebaked
Pinch of ground cinnamon	1½ tablespoons butter
¼ teaspoon almond extract	

Preheat the oven to 350 degrees F. Combine the flour and sugars; mix well. Add the cinnamon, extracts, and cherries. Pour into a pastry shell and dot with butter. Cover with a lattice top. (If you like, you can sprinkle the lattice top with a mixture of granulated sugar and cinnamon.) Bake for 45 minutes.

6 to 8 servings

BLUEBERRY PIE

1 deep-dish pie shell, fully
   cooked
4 cups (2 pints) fresh whole
   blueberries, washed and
   thoroughly drained
14 tablespoons sugar

½ cup water
1½ tablespoons lemon juice
2 tablespoons flour
1 cup whipping cream
2 tablespoons powdered sugar

Bake the pie shell according to package directions and set aside to cool. In a 1½-quart stainless-steel saucepan, combine 1 cup of the blueberries with the sugar, water, lemon juice, and flour. Stirring constantly, bring the mixture to a quick boil over high heat. Reduce the heat to medium and continue to cook for 5 to 10 minutes. When the sauce is thick and glossy, remove from the heat and transfer to a large bowl to cool. Ensure that the remaining berries are thoroughly dry, then spoon them into the pastry shell, mounding slightly in the middle. Pour cooled blueberry sauce over the berries.

With an electric mixer, whip the cream in a cold mixing bowl until it begins to thicken. Beat in the powdered sugar, and continue beating until the cream forms peaks on the beaters when they are lifted out of the bowl. Spoon the whipped cream into a pastry bag fitted with a decorative tip and pipe a border around the edge of the pie. Serve at once.

6 to 8 servings

Peach Pandowdy

4½	cups peeled, sliced peaches (about 2¼ pounds)		1	cup yellow cornmeal
¼	cup plus 3 tablespoons brown sugar		1½	teaspoons baking soda
¼	cup plus 3 tablespoons granulated sugar		½	teaspoon salt
2	teaspoons fresh lemon juice		1	egg, lightly beaten
¼	teaspoon ground nutmeg		½	cup light cream
1	teaspoon ground cinnamon		1	tablespoon vanilla extract
¼	teaspoon ground allspice		1½	teaspoons peach brandy
5	tablespoons melted butter		5	tablespoons granulated sugar mixed with 2 tablespoons ground cinnamon

Preheat the oven to 350 degrees F. In a medium bowl, combine the peaches with the sugars (reserve 3 tablespoons of the brown sugar for later use), lemon juice, nutmeg, cinnamon, allspice, and 3 tablespoons of the melted butter. Arrange the peaches in a large flameproof ceramic or glass baking dish.

In a medium bowl, sift together the dry ingredients plus the remaining 3 tablespoons of brown sugar. Stir in the egg, cream, vanilla, and a tablespoon of the remaining melted butter; mix until just combined. Pour the batter over the peaches and bake for approximately 30 minutes or until the bread batter is cooked through. Combine the peach brandy and the remaining melted butter. In a separate bowl, combine the sugar and cinnamon. Remove the pandowdy from the oven. Brush the top with the brandy-butter mixture. Sprinkle with the sugar-cinnamon mixture and broil 5 inches from the heat for 1 or 2 minutes. Serve with French vanilla ice cream.

6 to 8 servings

PEACH PIE

1	9-inch pie shell		1½	teaspoons ground nutmeg

1   9-inch pie shell
    Pastry dough for 1 pie shell
8   ripe peaches, peeled, pitted,
        and cut into ½-inch slices
1   teaspoon vanilla extract
¼   teaspoon almond extract
1   cup granulated sugar
¾   cup packed brown sugar
¼   cup all-purpose flour
¼   teaspoon salt
2   tablespoons lemon juice
¼   cup (½ stick) butter
1   teaspoon ground cinnamon

1½ teaspoons ground nutmeg
2   tablespoons granulated sugar mixed
        with 1 teaspoon ground
        cinnamon
¼   cup packed brown sugar
2   tablespoons flour
3   tablespoons butter
¾   teaspoon ground cinnamon
1   cup whipping cream, whipped
1   teaspoon grated orange peel
1   tablespoon fresh orange juice
1   tablespoon orange brandy

Preheat the oven to 350 degrees F. In a large ceramic bowl, combine the peaches, extracts, sugars, flour, salt and lemon juice. Allow to stand in the bowl undisturbed for 10 to 15 minutes, then drain the peaches, reserving the liquid. Arrange the peaches in the pie shell and dot with the butter. Sprinkle the filling with the cinnamon and nutmeg. Add enough of the reserved liquid to just cover the fruit. Set aside the remaining liquid for later use. Roll the remaining pastry into a 10-inch circle. Sprinkle the cinnamon-sugar mixture over the pastry circle and lightly press into the dough. Cut the pastry into ten strips ¾ inch wide and arrange in a lattice pattern over the filling. Trim strips 1 inch from the rim of the pie plate; fold the trimmed edges under the lower crust, pinching to seal.

In a small bowl, mix ¼ cup brown sugar with 2 tablespoons flour, 3 tablespoons butter, and ¾ teaspoon cinnamon until crumbly. Without packing, spoon this mixture into the open spaces of the latticework. Place the pie on a baking sheet and bake until the crust is golden, approximately 40 minutes. During baking, baste occasionally with any juices that run over and with the reserved liquid. Cool on a rack for 2 hours. Serve with the whipped cream combined with the grated orange peel, orange juice, and brandy.

6 to 8 servings

Apple Pie

1   9-inch pie shell
    Dough for 1 pie shell
6   cups Granny Smith apples,
       cored, peeled, and sliced
       ⅛ inch thick
1   tablespoon fresh lemon juice
½   cup granulated sugar
¼   cup brown sugar

1   teaspoon ground cinnamon
¼   teaspoon ground allspice
¼   teaspoon ground nutmeg
⅛   teaspoon ground cloves
1   tablespoon flour
2   tablespoons butter, cut into small
       pieces

Preheat the oven to 350 degrees F. In a large bowl, combine the apples, lemon juice, sugars, spices, and flour. Mix well and transfer to the pie shell. Mound high in the middle of the shell, because the apples will shrink during cooking. Dot with the butter. Cut the pastry into ten strips ¾ inch wide and arrange in a lattice pattern over the filling. Trim the strips 1 inch from rim of pie plate; fold trimmed edges under the lower crust, pinching to seal. Place in the preheated oven and bake for 40 to 50 minutes. Cool on rack for 2 hours and serve.

6 to 8 servings

OLD-FASHIONED BUTTERMILK PIE

1	unbaked pie shell	⅓	cup butter, melted and slightly cooled
2	large eggs	½	cup buttermilk
1½	cups sugar	1	tablespoon lemon juice
1	tablespoon flour		

Preheat the oven to 450 degrees F. Beat the eggs and sugar together. Add the flour, butter, and buttermilk. Finally, add the lemon juice. Mix well and pour into the pie shell. Place pie in oven and reduce temperature to 340 degrees F. Bake for 45 minutes to 1 hour or until a knife inserted into the middle of the pie comes out clean.

6 to 8 servings

CHESS PIE

1	8-inch unbaked pie shell	2	teaspoons flour
½	cup (1 stick) butter, melted	2	tablespoons cornmeal
1¼	cups sugar	1	tablespoon lemon juice
3	whole eggs, slightly beaten	⅛	teaspoon almond extract
½	cup half-and-half		

Preheat the oven to 350 degrees F. Combine the butter and sugar. Add the eggs, beating on slow mixing speed. Add the half-and-half, flour, cornmeal, lemon juice, and almond extract; beat well. Pour into the pie shell. Bake for 40 minutes or until firm; the pie is done when a butter knife inserted in the center comes out clean.

6 to 8 servings

BEST-EVER CHOCOLATE CHIP COOKIES

2	cups butter	2	tablespoons ground cinnamon
2	cups granulated sugar	2	teaspoons ground nutmeg
2	cups brown sugar	⅛	teaspoon cayenne pepper
4	cups flour	4	eggs
2	teaspoons baking soda	2	teaspoons baking powder
5	cups oatmeal, processed in a blender to a fine powder	1	cup chopped walnuts
		1½	cups chopped macadamia nuts
24	ounces chocolate chips	½	cup toasted sunflower seeds
1	teaspoon salt	1	tablespoon vanilla extract

Preheat the oven to 375 degrees F. Cream the butter and both sugars. Add the remaining ingredients and mix well. Roll into ¾-inch balls and place 2 inches apart on an ungreased cookie sheet. Bake for 10 minutes.

Yields 112 cookies

PECAN PUFFS

½	cup (1 stick) butter, softened	1	tablespoon vanilla extract
1	tablespoon cream cheese, softened	1	cup coarsely ground pecans
2	tablespoons granulated sugar	1	cup cake flour, sifted
			Powdered sugar

Preheat the oven to 300 degrees F. Cream the butter and cream cheese until fluffy. Add the sugars and vanilla. Cream until light and fluffy. Mix the pecans and flour together and stir into the butter mixture.

Roll into small balls and place on a lightly greased baking sheet. Bake for 45 minutes. Allow the cookies to cool slightly. While the cookies are still warm, roll them in powdered sugar. Allow cookies to cool completely and roll in powdered sugar again.

4½ to 5 dozen

FRESH BLACKBERRY COBBLER WITH CHANTILLY CREAM

3 cups fresh blackberries
1 cup all-purpose flour
2 teaspoons double-acting
   baking powder
1 cup sugar

2 eggs
¾ cup half-and-half
2 teaspoons vanilla extract
2 tablespoons sugar
1 teaspoon ground nutmeg

Preheat the oven to 350 degrees F. Place the blackberries in a colander and wash under cold running water. Pick over the berries, removing stems and blemished berries. Spread the berries on an absorbent towel and pat dry with another towel. Lightly butter a 2-quart oven proof soufflé or casserole dish. Place the berries in the dish and set aside.

In another large bowl, sift together the flour and baking powder. Add the sugar, eggs, half-and-half, and vanilla extract. Beat briskly with a wooden spoon until thoroughly combined and then pour over the berries. Combine the 2 tablespoons of sugar and teaspoon of ground nutmeg and lightly sprinkle over the top of the batter. Bake for 1 hour or until the top is crusty brown. When done, remove the cobbler from the oven and allow to cool. While the cobbler is cooling, you may prepare the Chantilly Cream (below).

CHANTILLY CREAM

1 cup chilled whipping cream
1 tablespoon superfine sugar

¾ teaspoon vanilla extract

In a chilled stainless-steel bowl, beat the cream, sugar, and vanilla until firm peaks form. Cover and chill for up to 3 hours ahead of time. Rewhisk if necessary.

6 to 8 servings

FRIED PEACHES

3	large, firm peaches	¼	teaspoon ground cinnamon
3	tablespoons unsalted butter	3	tablespoons brandy
5	tablespoons sugar		

In a large pot, bring enough water to a boil to completely cover the peaches. Allow the peaches to boil over high heat for 2 to 3 minutes. Remove the peaches to a colander to cool and drain. When peaches are cool enough to handle, peel them with a paring knife, cut in half, and remove the pits. Place the peaches flat side down on an absorbent towel to dry. In a 10-inch stainless-steel skillet, begin melting the butter over medium heat. Add the sugar and cinnamon, and stir constantly until the butter is completely melted. Add the peaches, flat side down, and cook uncovered for 2 to 3 minutes, or until the bottoms of the peaches are golden. Turn the peaches over, baste with pan juices, and cook for an additional 2 to 3 minutes. Warm the brandy in a large spoon or ladle; carefully ignite it with a match and pour it over the peaches. Gently slide the pan in a circular motion over the heat until the flames die and serve immediately, either alone, over vanilla ice cream, or with pound cake and vanilla ice cream

3 to 6 servings

RICE PUDDING

1	cup water	2	teaspoons vanilla extract
¼	teaspoon salt	⅛	teaspoon almond extract
½	cup raw rice	½	cup raisins
1	quart half-and-half	1	tablespoon ground cinnamon
¼	cup (½ stick) butter	⅛	teaspoon ground allspice
3	eggs, well beaten	4	teaspoons sugar
½	cup sugar		

Combine the water and salt. Bring to a boil. Add the rice. Do not stir. Cover tightly and cook for 7 minutes. Add the half-and-half and butter. Stir, bring to a boil, cover, and cook over low heat for 1 hour. Beat together the eggs, sugar, and extracts. Pour into the rice mixture, stirring slowly until the mixture thickens. Finally, add raisins. In a separate bowl, combine the cinnamon, allspice, and sugar. Serve the pudding warm or cold with cinnamon-sugar sprinkled on top. Keep any leftover pudding refrigerated.

6 servings

BERRIES AND CREAM

1	cup fresh raspberries		½	pint vanilla ice cream
1	cup fresh ripe strawberries		½	cup heavy cream
½	cup powdered sugar		¼	teaspoon vanilla extract
½	cup Grand Marnier liqueur			Toasted almond slivers

Wash the raspberries; hull and wash the strawberries. Drain and pat dry. Place in a large serving bowl and sprinkle with the sugar and liqueur. Toss gently and chill for 1 hour, stirring occasionally. Soften the ice cream at room temperature for 1 hour. Beat the heavy cream until stiff. Add the extract. Fold the cream into the softened ice cream. Add the berries, blend gently, and serve immediately. Garnish with toasted almond slivers.

4 servings

DAMSON ICE CREAM

6	large egg yolks		⅓	cup boiling water
2⅓	cups sugar		¾	cups sugar
3	cups half-and-half		2	tablespoons cornstarch
½	teaspoon salt		2	tablespoons butter
3	cups damson plums, pitted and quartered		3½	cups heavy cream
			4	teaspoons vanilla extract

In the top of a double boiler set over simmering water combine the egg yolks, 2⅓ cups sugar, the half-and-half, and ¼ teaspoon of the salt. Cook the mixture, stirring constantly, until it can coat the back of the spoon—but do not let it boil. Transfer the custard to a large bowl, covering it with buttered waxed paper. Chill until cold.

In a large saucepan, combine the damsons and ⅓ cup boiling water. Bring the water to a second boil, reduce the heat, and simmer the mixture, stirring, for 3 minutes. In a bowl, combine the remaining ¾ cup sugar, the cornstarch, and the remaining ¼ teaspoon salt. Bring the damson mixture to a boil, add the sugar mixture, and simmer, stirring, until slightly thickened. Remove the pan from the heat, stir in the butter, and let the mixture cool. Stir the cream, vanilla, and damson mixture into the custard and stir until combined well. Transfer the mixture to an ice cream freezer and freeze it according to the manufacturer's instructions.

Yields about 2½ quarts

PEACH ICE CREAM

1¼	pounds unpeeled peaches	¾	cup sugar
¼	cup fresh lemon juice	2	egg yolks
2	cups half-and-half		

Blanch the peaches in a large pot of boiling water for 1 minute; peel. Purée the peach pulp with the lemon juice in processor or blender; you need 2 cups. Refrigerate until ready to use. Simmer the half-and-half in a heavy, medium saucepan for 20 minutes, stirring frequently; do not boil. Add the sugar and stir until dissolved.

Whisk the yolks to blend in a bowl. Gradually whisk in the cream mixture. Pour this back into the saucepan and whisk over medium-low heat until the mixture thickens enough to coat the back of a spoon. Do not boil. Strain the custard and cool. Blend the custard and peach purée. Chill overnight if possible. Transfer to an ice cream maker and process according to the manufacturer's directions.

Yields 1 pint

RASPBERRY ICE CREAM

7	cups half-and-half	3	cups sugar
1	vanilla bean	¼	cup vanilla extract
1	dozen egg yolks	1	quart heavy cream
½	teaspoon salt	1½	pints raspberries

In a large saucepan, combine the half-and-half and vanilla bean. Scald. In a large bowl, beat the egg yolks until light and bright yellow. Add the salt. Remove the vanilla bean from the milk mixture. Stirring constantly, pour about half of the half-and-half mixture over the eggs. Blend well and return the mixture to the saucepan. Add the sugar and stir continuously as the mixture cooks over medium heat. Cook until the mixture is thick enough to coat a spoon. Chill in the refrigerator. When chilled, add the vanilla extract, heavy cream, and raspberries. Mix and freeze using 2 parts cracked ice to 1 part salt, or according to the manufacturer's directions.

Yields 3 quarts

STRAWBERRY ICE CREAM

¾ cup sugar	1 tablespoon vanilla extract
1 tablespoon flour	½ cup milk
⅛ teaspoon salt	1 cup half-and-half
2 cups half-and-half	1½ cups heavy cream
7 egg yolks, slightly beaten	3 cups strawberries

Mix together the sugar, flour, and salt. Stir in the 2 cups of half-and-half and mix well. In the top of a double boiler, cook the custard, stirring constantly, until slightly thickened. Cover and allow to cook for 10 minutes longer.

In a separate bowl, beat the egg yolks. Stir some of the hot milk mixture into the eggs, then add the eggs back to the milk mixture. Cook this over the double boiler for 5 minutes, stirring constantly, or until the mixture can coat a spoon. Chill for 2 hours.

Add the vanilla extract, milk, 1 cup of half-and-half, heavy cream, and strawberries. Mix well and freeze using 2 parts cracked ice to 1 part salt, or according to the manufacturer's directions.

Yields 1½ quarts

PEPPERMINT ICE CREAM

1 tablespoon flour	1 cup light cream
⅛ teaspoon salt	3 cups crushed peppermint candy
2 cups half-and-half	2 drops red food coloring, optional
7 egg yolks, slightly beaten	
1 tablespoon peppermint extract	

Mix together the flour and salt. Stir in the 2 cups of half-and-half and mix well. In the top of a double boiler, cook the mixture, stirring constantly, until slightly thickened. Cover and allow to cook 10 minutes longer.

In a separate bowl, beat the egg yolks. Stir some of the hot half-and-half mixture into the eggs, then add the eggs back to the half-and-half mixture; mix well. Cook this mixture over the double boiler for 5 minutes, stirring constantly, or until it can coat a spoon. Chill for 2 hours.

Add the mint extract, light cream, peppermint candy, and food coloring; mix well and freeze using 2 parts cracked ice to 1 part salt, or according to the manufacturer's directions.

Yields 1½ pints

VANILLA ICE CREAM

1	quart heavy cream	8	egg yolks
1	vanilla bean, split open	⅛	teaspoon salt
1¼	cups sugar	¼	cup vanilla extract

In the top of a double boiler, combine the cream and vanilla bean. Scald the cream. When tiny beads form around the outer edges of the cream add the sugar, do not allow the cream to boil. Remove the vanilla bean from the pot and let it cool enough to handle. Scrape the beans from the pod into the cream mixture. Discard the bean pod. Stir until the sugar dissolves.

Beat the egg yolks until thick and creamy. Gradually add the sugar-cream mixture to the eggs, beating well to make a custard. Stir in the salt and extract. Chill and keep refrigerated until ready to use. Freeze using 2 parts cracked ice to 1 part rock salt, or follow the manufacturer's directions.

Yields 1 quart

THE LEGACY AND LESSONS OF HAMPTON

"At Hampton I got my first taste of what it meant to live a life of unselfishness, my knowledge of the fact that the happiest individuals are those who do the most to make others useful and happy. . . . At Hampton I . . . learned to love labour, not alone for its financial value, but for labour's own sake and for the independence and self-reliance which the ability to do something which the world wants done brings. . . ."

Those lessons were learned firsthand from teachers such as Mary Mackie and General Armstrong himself: "In all my career at Hampton, and ever since I have been out in the world, Miss Mackie, the head teacher to whom I have referred, proved one of my strongest and most helpful friends. Her advice and encouragement were always helpful and encouraging to me in the darkest hour. . . . Miss Mackie was a member of one of the oldest and most cultured families of the North, and yet for two weeks she worked by my side cleaning windows, dusting rooms, putting beds in order. . . . She took the greatest satisfaction in helping to clean them herself. . . . It was hard for me to understand how a woman of [Miss Mackie's] education and social standing could take such delight in . . . service."

At the age of twenty-seven Samuel C. Armstrong embarked on a life's work that not only produced a legacy, but also set the example for those he led from the ignorance of slavery into the light of education and self reliance. His words of wisdom and exemplary life touched the hands, minds, and hearts of all with whom he came into contact, including Booker T. Washington. He provided an education for life and a desire to embark on a life of service:

"I never saw a man who so completely lost sight of himself. I do not believe he ever had a selfish thought. [General Armstrong] was just as happy in trying to assist some other institution in the South as he was working for Hampton. . . ."

—Booker T. Washington, Hampton, Class of 1875

"Was I heah when dey start Hampton? O yes! Lawd chile! I was heah when de Gen'l say, 'let's make a school.' . . . You see when dey close up de Civil War, den dey start up Hampton."

—Mrs. Matilda B. Laws (b. 1854)

245

Courses of Study.

The courses of study embrace three years, and include—

NORMAL COURSE.

- *Language.*—Spelling, Reading, Sentence-Making, English Grammar, Analysis, Rhetoric, Composition, Elocution.
- *Mathematics.*—Mental Arithmetic, Written Arithmetic, Algebra, Geometry, Mathematical Drawing.
- *History.*—History of United States, History of England—Readings from English writers. Universal History.
- *Natural Science.*—Geography—Map-drawing, Physical Geography, Natural History, Natural Philosophy, Physiology, Botany.
- *Miscellaneous.*—Science of Civil Government, Moral Science, Bible Lessons, Drill in Teaching, Principles of Business, Vocal Training, Instrumental Music.

AGRICULTURAL COURSE.

Studies of the Normal Course at discretion. Lectures on the following courses: Formation of Soils, Rotation of Crops, Management of Stock, Fruit Culture, Cultivation of Crops, Drainage, Market Gardening, Meteorology, Practical Instruction in the routine of Farming and Market Gardening.

COMMERCIAL COURSE.

Studies of the Normal Course at discretion. Instruction in Book-keeping, Single and Double Entry, in Business Letters, Contracts, Account of Sales, and other Business and Legal Papers, and in Commercial Law. Each student is required to keep his account current with the Institute in proper form.

MECHANICAL COURSE.

Studies of the Normal Course at discretion. Practical Instruction in the different varieties of Sewing-Machines in use, in household industries, and in the following: Penmanship, Free Hand Drawing, Mechanical Drawing, Printing.

Lectures are given through the year on Agricultural topics. Arrangements are being made to secure every year the services of leading literary and scientific men in a Lecture Course that shall afford the highest order of entertainment and instruction.

EXPENSES AND LABOR.

- Board, per month, ... $8.00
- Washing and lights, per month, ... 1.00
- Fuel, per month, ... .75
- Use of furniture, per month, ... .25
- $10.00

Clothing and books extra, to be paid for in cash.

Able-bodied young men and women over eighteen years of age are expected to pay half in cash and half in work; that is, $5 per month in cash, and to work out the balance. Boys and girls of eighteen years and less are required to pay $6 per month. *Students are held responsible for all balances against them that they may not have worked out.*

The amount of profitable labor being limited, it is desired to extend its advantages as far as possible; hence only those who are absolutely unable to pay any thing in cash are allowed to work out their whole expenses. Young men and women, whose parents desire that they shall not be taken out of school to work, may, upon the payment of $10 per month, attend school without interruption, but will nevertheless be required to work on Saturdays, at such hours as may be assigned them. LABOR IS REQUIRED OF ALL, for purposes of discipline and instruction. To this end, day scholars are expected to labor at the rate of an hour per day, at such industries as may be assigned them.

Bills are made out and are payable at the end of the month. The regular cash payment is to be *monthly, in advance.*

The regular annual tuition fee of the institution is seventy dollars. Students are not required to pay this. As the amount has to be secured by the Trustees, by solicitation among the friends of education, students are called upon annually to write letters to their benefactors.

DISCIPLINE.

Courtesy and mutual forbearance are expected of both pupils and teachers, as indispensable to good discipline.

Every student is by enrollment committed to the discipline and regulations of the school.

Students are subject to suspension or discharge for an unsatisfactory course in respect to study, conduct, or labor.

The use of ardent spirits and tobacco is prohibited. Letter-writing is subject to regulation.

The wardrobes of all students are subject to inspection and regulation by the proper officers.

Students are subject to drill and guard duty. Obedience to the Commandant must be implicit. The rights of students are properly guarded.

DAILY ORDER OF EXERCISES AT THE H. N. AND A. INSTITUTE.

- A.M.—5:00 Rising Bell.
- A.M.—5:45 Inspection of Men.
- A.M.—6:00 Breakfast.
- A.M.—6:30 Family Prayers.
- A.M.—8:00 Inspection of quarters.
- A.M.—8:30 Opening of school. Roll Call and Exercises.
- A.M.—8:55 to 10:20 Classes in Reading, Natural Philosophy, Arithmetic, Grammar, Geography, and Book-keeping.
- A.M.—10:20 to 10:40 Recess.
- A.M.—10:40 to 12:15 Classes in Writing, Arithmetic, Grammar, History, Algebra, and Elocution.
- P.M.—12:15 to 1:30 Dinner and intermission.
- P.M.—1:30 Roll Call.
- P.M.—1:40 to 2:50 Classes in Spelling, Arithmetic, Grammar, Geography, Natural Philosophy, History, Civil Government, and Moral Science.
- P.M.—4:00 Cadet Drill.
- P.M.—6:00 Supper.
- P.M.—6:45 Evening Prayers.
- P.M.—7:15 to 9:00 Evening Study Hours.
- P.M.—9:30 Retiring Bell.

On Sunday there are morning religious services in the Chapel, conducted by the Rev. Richard Tolman, formerly of Tewksbury, Mass., who has pastoral charge of the school. The Church is organized as the "Bethesda Church," and has no denominational name or connection. Sunday afternoon there are Bible-Classes in the Assembly Hall, and in the evening a lecture or prayer-meeting.

Tribute to Samuel C. Armstrong

". . . I have spoken of the impression that was made upon me by the buildings and general appearance of the Hampton Institute, but I have not spoken of that which made the greatest and most lasting impression upon me, and that was a great man—General S. C. Armstrong was . . . the rarest, strongest, and most beautiful character that it has been my privilege to meet. . . . It has been my fortune to meet personally many of what are called great characters, both in Europe and America, but I do not hesitate to say that I never met any man who . . . was the equal of General Armstrong. . . . One might have removed from Hampton all the buildings, classrooms, teachers, and industries, and given the men and women there the opportunity of coming into daily contact with General Armstrong, and that alone would have been a liberal education. . . ."

—Booker T. Washington, Hampton, Class of 1875

BIBLIOGRAPHY

Armstrong, M. F., and Helen W. Ludlow. *Hampton and Its Students by Two of Its Teachers.* New York: G. P. Putnam's Sons, 1874.

Dawson, Martha E. *Hampton University: A National Treasure.* Silver Spring, Md.: Venture Books Beckham House Publishers, 1994.

The Hampton Album, The Museum of Modern Art. New York, 1966.

Hampton Graduates 1871–1899, Institute publication.

Howe, Albert. "*Memories of Old Hampton.*" *Daily Press Newport,* March 19, 1925.

Lindsey, Doual F. *Indians at Hampton Institute 1877–1923.* Urbana, Ill.: University of Illinois Press, 1995.

Lyford, Carrie Alberta. *A Book of Recipes for the Cooking School.* Hampton, Va.: Press of the Hampton Normal and Agricultutral Institute, 1921.

Moton, Robert Russa. *Finding a Way Out: An Autobiography.* Garden City, N.Y.: Doubleday, Page & Co., 1921.

Peabody, Frances G. *Education for Life, the Story of Hampton Institute.* Garden City, N.Y.: Doubleday, Page & Co., 1918.

Perdue, Charles L. Jr., Thomas E. Barden, and Robert K. Phillips, eds. *Weevils in the Wheat: Interviews with Virginia Ex-slaves.* Bloomington and London: Indiana University Press, 1976.

Pleasant, Mae Barbes Boone. *Hampton University Our Home by the Sea.* Virginia Beach, Va.: Donning Company, 1992.

Robinson, William Hannibal. "A History of Hampton," submitted in partial fulfillment of the requirement for the degree of Doctor of Philosophy in the School of Education of New York University, 1953, accepted October 12, 1954.

Stensvaag, James T., ed. *Hampton From the Sea to the Stars.* Virginia Beach, Va.: Donning Company, 1985.

Talbot, Edith Armstrong. *Samuel Armstrong: A Biographical Study.* New York: Doubleday, Page & Co., 1904.

Subject Index

RECIPE INDEX